For HANDMADE Christmas

Handmade for Christmas is an original work, first published in 2012 in the United Kingdom by Future Publishing Limited in magazine form under the title *Handmade Christmas*. This title is printed and distributed in North America under license. All rights reserved.

ISBN 978-1-57421-508-3

Printed in China
First printing

HANDMADE
For Christmas

Easy Crafts and Creative Ideas for Sewing, Stitching, Papercraft, Knitting, and Crochet

Editors of Future Publishing

Design Originals

an Imprint of Fox Chapel Publishing

www.d-originals.com

HANDMADE for Christmas

72

32

44

Start crafting here...

24

66

28

22

58

Designers
homestyle

CRAFTS TO CROSS STITCH

CRAFTS TO KNIT

Welcome!

to *Handmade For Christmas!* This wonderful collection of ideas and projects will keep you crafting through the festive season and beyond! Christmastime is a great time to try out a new craft or to brush up on old skills. Dust off that sewing machine, free that yarn from storage, and find that stash of festive papers to start creating beautiful decorations for your home and gifts for your family and friends. Giving handmade gifts tells your loved ones that you care enough to spend time making them something special.

What child wouldn't love counting down the days until Christmas with the **knitted advent calendar on page 79?** It's a great project to use up leftover yarn. Need some new decorations to spruce up your home for the holidays? The **Christmas Chic cushion on page 60** is just the thing to make your family and guests feel welcome.

You will also find ideas on decorating with baubles, creating a white Christmas indoors, and how to add some retro charm to your style by mixing vintage prints with modern colors and embellishments. If you like to get the family involved in the crafting, grab the kids and paint some holiday cards and decorations, or send them outside to gather some twigs and pinecones to add a natural touch to your décor. Whatever your style, you will have no shortage of ideas and creative inspiration to have a truly wonderful handmade Christmas.

INTRODUCTION
Christmas Style

CREATIVE IDEAS FOR A PERSONALIZED HOLIDAY LOOK

WISHING YOU A
merry
CHRISTMAS

Blend neutral fabric colors with natural materials – you'll create a calming festive room scheme that's simplicity itself...

Nature Chic

Muted colors and natural textures combine for a beautiful Christmas look that's not only perfect for contemporary homes, but also a breeze to create from scratch

I f you're after a timeless, classic look for your Christmas décor, it doesn't get much simpler than this natural look. Choose traditional festive motifs, such as stars, angels and reindeers, and create them in neutral tones of cream, café latte, white and trendy pale grey. Stick to these simple motifs and colors and you can craft stunning decorations that can be brought out and used year after year, without ever showing signs of dating.

You can also approach the 'natural' theme by using unspoild materials and items from nature. Try pale shades of wood, paper, dried leaves, dried flowers and festive spices – these are all elements that can be put together in clever ways, for fuss-free decorations that smell divine, too!

The best fabrics for the natural look can vary, from delicate cream and white silk and voiles to more rustic hessians and calicos, depending on the particular style you want to take on. The simplicity of this look makes texture even more important, so faux fur is another great fabric; it can just be draped over chairs, or cut into large Christmas motifs to make a wooden floor feel more cozy. In the same way, embellishments could include pretty cream buttons and white velvet ribbons, or perhaps hemp cord, natural string and slate textured buttons – it's really up to you!

Whatever you decide, there's no need to break the bank – to craft this look.

Familiar motifs, such as these three-dimensional reindeer heads, are given a new twist worked in whites

Image: Cox & Cox

Place natural items such as delicate branches in a tall, white vase for a classic, understated look

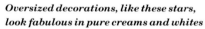

Oversized decorations, like these stars, look fabulous in pure creams and whites

CINNAMON & LAVENDER
Decoration,
Pollyfields

TWIG & PEARL HEART WREATH
The Contemporary Home

Natural fabrics such as linen, wool and cotton add a soft, warm feel to your Christmas décor, and neutral colors are perfect for a welcoming and relaxing home. Add luxurious touches in velvet and tweed as embellishments, and use natural objects such as pebbles and driftwood for added interest. Finally, arrange ornaments in bowls on window sills and mantlepieces.

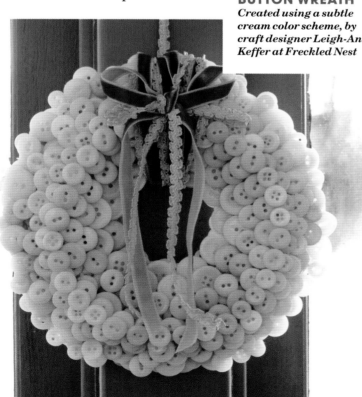

BUTTON WREATH
Created using a subtle cream color scheme, by craft designer Leigh-Ann Keffer at Freckled Nest

NEW IDEAS FOR NATURALS
5 ways to get the look

1. Cut simple natural shapes such as holly leaves from cream-colored felt, to decorate a wicker-style wreath.

2. Decorate your tree with white lights, then add handmade decorations in cream or grey. Attach ornaments with navy or grey velvet ribbon.

3. Spray some pine cones with white paint. Once dry, arrange in a large wooden bowl to make a stunning yet super-simple table centerpiece.

4. Photocopy music manuscripts or pages from children's Christmas books, then fold them into layered shapes to make ornaments.

5. Use crafter's wire to make 3D star shapes; cover them with layers of white tissue paper to make unique decorations, and pile them together.

Winter Wonderland

Chill out with a sparkling selection of icy blues, snowflake motifs and embellishments – you're guaranteed a white Christmas with this pretty frost-filled look

I nspired by the icy blues, shimmering silver and delicate textures of these stunning snow-filled interiors? Well, luckily, it's easy to give this style a handmade twist, whether you get clever with the decorations you buy, or want to rustle up your own crafty designs.

The secret of this Winter Wonderland look is that it's incredibly simple to create, whatever your budget, but the end results look highly impressive and rather sophisticated to boot! Forget applying fake snow onto window ledges – there are great ways to bring the chilly outdoor atmosphere into your home.

Keep your color palette limited with the palest blues, light greys and subtle sprinklings of silver glitter. Less is truly more with this look – add two many colors of glitter, for instance, and you'll end up with a multicolored, mismatched mess. Instead, gather some silver-patterned ribbon, plenty of white paper, vintage white, translucent and sparkling baubles, snowflake-patterned fabrics and white pom-pom trim and get making, interchanging the materials you use as you go for a fully coordinated look.

If you want to take things a little further, the delicate patterns of snowflakes lend themselves to a whole host of crafty decorations. Just remember not to overdo things – keep designs subtle and colors muted for a room scheme that will hang together so much better.

Bring a sparkling, frosty touch to your Christmas tree by coating the branches with a dusting of fake snow

Image: House of Fraser

Glittering highlights are key to creating a frosty festive look

Image: House of Fraser

Create a delicate look for your table settings by using clear and frosted baubles as place settings

Image: House of Fraser

Image: Marks & Spencer

seasonal sprinkle

To finish off your festive presents with a little sprinkle of rustic charm, simply attach one of these gorgeous 'Let It Snow' tags – they're sure to be a treat!
Let it snow gift tag, From The Wilde

Whip up a handmade snowstorm of your own, with our choice of cute snowflake presents and decorations

WINTER WARMER

This stunning tea cozy is lined and made with voiles and tyvek, and depending on the season chosen, may contain Angelina and merino wools. As every cozy is handmade, each will be slightly different, making a truly unique gift.
Winter Tea Cosy, From The Wilde

felted flurry

These gorgeous little felt decorations make a cute gift for a friend, or craft them for your own tree. They're available as a kit with all you need to make three fabulous snow ornaments – including cord, pre-cut felt pieces and thread.
Flurries Ornaments – Felt Appliqué Kit, Sew and So

STORMING AHEAD

Get those Christmas cards sorted now, to leave you with plenty more time for crafting presents! This navy snowstorm cut-out pearlized Christmas card comes with white envelope; the card is blank inside and would make the ideal companion to a homemade gift.
Navy snowstorm die-cut Christmas card, Dot Com Gift Shop

Retro Charm

Have a very vintage Christmas and plenty of old-fashioned festive fun using funky retro styles, mixing cool mid-20th-century prints with modern colors and embellishments.

The beauty of the current trend for retro décor is that the vintage vibe harks back to a simpler time, when to 'make do and mend' was the norm and Christmas homes were filled with handmade treasures that were passed down from generation to generation. And now things have come full circle as we adore the shabby-chic charm that such handmade items had, and try to recreate the look in our own homes – all of which makes this the perfect style for crafters of all abilities.

You don't have to look far to find what you need to conjure up a retro collection of decorations – upcycling old fabrics with bold prints and keeping an eye out for vintage toys, card or jewelry that you could use in a new way are all great places to start. Add a little glitter and you'll be ready to rock around the Christmas tree in next to no time!

Anything goes when it comes to the retro look, so it's up to you to choose the particular style you want to go for. Pick up some pretty cherry-red polkadot fabric, for instance, and combine it with retro floral prints to make stockings, bunting, banners and tree ornaments. Add a little pom-pom trim in a bright contrasting color and you're already nearly there! Bold felt shapes appliquéd onto geometric fabric prints are another sure-fire winner – go online and check out the many retro fabric stores on the web, and you're guaranteed to find something to spark your Christmas creativity.

Indulge yourself in pure nostalgia this Christmas with cute retro fabrics, gifts, wrap and decorations

Take inspiration from these crafty makes and buys to rustle up handmade decorations that have the vintage vibe...

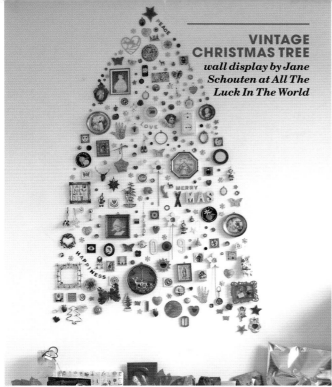

VINTAGE
CHRISTMAS TREE
wall display by Jane Schouten at All The Luck In The World

FESTIVE FIREPLACE
by Olga at Vintage Pretty

Whether you're planning on hand-crafting some retro-style decorations yourself, or are simply on the hunt for the most fabulous vintage festive finds you can buy – we've gathered together some cute and clever ideas for introducing a touch of vintage homespun charm into your home this Christmas.

UPCYCLED COMICS PAPERCHAIN
Ellie Ellie

IDEAS TO TRY
5 easy ways to go retro...

1. Recycle and re-use vintage shop finds and turn them into a unique display – simply made by hanging retro buys together in a tree shape!

2. Make use of any old snow globes you have. Group them together for a kitsch, nostalgic centerpiece.

3. Oversized pom-poms make for a novel multicolored garland, so you can deck the halls with a quirky look.

4. Make a unique festive wreath by gluing together a mixture of colorful second-hand glass baubles – the more vintage, the better. Simply attach them to a circular wood base and top with a flouncy bow.

5. Upcycle vintage Christmas cards by framing the card fronts and hanging them vertically from some polkadot ribbon to create an instant display.

For more vintage inspiration, sit down and enjoy a classic black-and-white movie, such as It's a Wonderful Life

It's fine to mismatch bold prints with this look – in fact, the quirkier the result, the better!

Second-hand shops and garage sales can often reveal hidden treasure troves of vintage Christmas memorabilia, which can then be revived and reused by savvy crafters

Brilliant Baubles

Nothing shouts Christmas louder than baubles, and there are so many ways to give them a personalized spin. Just pick your method and roll with it...

W hether you fancy making your own, giving some existing ones an upgrade or simply finding fresh ways to display them, baubles and other hanging festive ornaments are the ideal way to customize your Christmas.

We've explored just some of the possibilities on the following pages so you can let your imagination run wild!

Main photo: Ikea

Selection of baubles from Ikea

Traditional baubles look elegant sitting in a bowl

Give your baubles a crafty twist – these fabulous felt ones are bold, bright and wonderfully tactile

WONDERFUL WAYS WITH BAUBLES

TAKE THE COOKIE
Some Christmas decs look good enough to eat, so why not make yours edible? Cookies cut into festive shapes look great strung on twine and hung about the house. Or get baking your own gingerbread shapes and decorate with simple white piped icing. Just be prepared that they won't be hanging around for long!

You could also make them from non-edible salt dough to prevent them from disappearing.

BLOW YOUR OWN RETRO COLORS
Why not make some vintage-inspired felt baubles like these (top right)? You can tailor the colors to match your décor, and they're simple enough to get your whole family making them.

EASY UPDATES
If you'd prefer to give upcycling a go, you could customize old baubles from Christmas past using acrylic paint.

Acrylic paint is also a great idea for personalizing baubles with names and dates – just hang them up to dry to avoid smudges.

Or, you can use watercolor paints if you want to update the details each year – just wash with soap and warm water to remove them at the end of the festive season.

CHILD'S PLAY
If you'd like to get the kids involved, pom-poms that can be hung as baubles are always a popular make for young children – and there are many handy tutorials online if you need a refresher on how to make them.

ON THE WIRE
Dainty baubles can get lost amid the pine needles, so why not dangle yours from a vintage birdcage or wirework chandelier? Go for coordinating colors, or create an eclectic mix of baubles and other ornaments of varying sizes and styles.

HOW TO MAKE 3D DOILY DECS
Create these pretty 3D paper baubles in about 15 minutes.

What you need:
- Small paper doilies
- Natural hemp cord
- Glue

1 Take five paper doilies and fold them in half.

2 Cut a length of brown hemp string.

3 Stick the doilies together side by side. Trap the hemp string in the middle before sticking the last pair together.

Photos, clockwise from left: Ikea, House of Fraser, Hobbycraft, Cox & Cox

Above left: Selection of baubles from Ikea

Above right: Hang baubles from a garland for a sumptuous look

PERFECT PLACEMENT

Traditional baubles look elegant in a bowl , piled in a vase or simply laid out in a dish like foil-wrapped sweets. Single baubles can add an extra-special touch to Christmas table place settings – thread them onto some thin ribbon or metallic cord and then tie around a folded napkin, so the bow and bauble rest on top for a pretty decorative effect.

MAKE AN IMPACT

Baubles always look pretty hung from silky ribbons in front of windows, from mantelpieces and even from empty picture frames – making them practically a work of art! Group them at varying heights in rows, or bunch together like an upside-down bouquet for optimum impact.

You can also place clusters of baubles on windowsills and mantelpieces for dramatic effect – make sure they don't roll off and smash by weaving them through a few sprigs from your Christmas tree. Have some fun experimenting with different displays and styles – baubles are so versatile that the possibilities are endless.

HOW TO DECOUPAGE OLD ORNAMENTS

Following this step-by-step guide, you can upcycle your old baubles in about 20 minutes.

What you need:
- Old baubles
- Bright doilies
- Bright tissue paper sheets
- Bright organza ribbons
- Glue

1 Cut a length of ribbon and thread onto an ornament.

2 Cut the doilies and tear the tissue paper into small pieces.

3 Randomly stick the squares onto the bauble with glue, overlapping edges. Coat the finished bauble with a thin layer of glue. Hang them on a clothing rack or similar to dry.

Festive Family Fun

Gather your little ones around the craft table and give this year's Christmas decorations the personal touch, while also having some festive family fun…

I t's no secret that kids absolutely love making Christmas decorations and cards. It might get messy, especially when paint is involved, but the end results often look brilliant and serve as an enduring memento. From handprint decorations, to thumbprint fairylights and potato-printed penguins, here are some crafty ideas to get you started. So grab your paints and the nearest child and off you go…

HANDPRINTED BAUBLES

Who'd have thought that little hands were capable of producing a row of cute festive snowmen? To recreate this fabulous effect, pull up the sleeves of the nearest child and paint their hand with non-toxic acrylic paint (the little bottles from craft stores are easier to clean off than the thick artists' variety). With their palm on the base, ask them to grasp the ornament like they're holding a ball. Lift the ornament away and balance on an empty egg carton to dry. Repeat for as many baubles or children as necessary! Once dry, draw in the snowmen detail – buttons, scarves, faces and hats – with different colored permanent pens.

THUMBPRINT FAIRY LIGHTS

We love this string of fairy lights made from tiny thumbprints (opposite, top left). The more colors the better when you're making this design, which works brilliantly on big posters or smaller greetings cards.

Squeeze small amounts of different colored washable paints into individual pots and help smaller children make a row of different colored prints. Older kids won't need much guidance here and, once dry, will be able to draw in their own strings with black pen. If you've got the time for some more festive creativity, try making thumbprint wreaths or Christmas trees in green paint, adding detail with pens.

POTATO-PRINT PENGUIN CARDS

Potato-printing brings back memories of plastic aprons in an 80s nursery setting, but as a technique it's a fantastically creative way to make your own designs – kids just love that there's more to potatoes than chips. The simple penguin designs (opposite) are made

from two different size slices, cut from a potato. You can make loads of quick cards in a couple of sittings with really effective results.

First, choose two potatoes, one larger than the other, to fit your card blanks – brown cardstock provides a great background texture, but white will work

Photo credit: Jill Dubien

*Quick, fun and easy –
cute fairylights*

*The humble
potato is a tiny
crafter's best
friend, making
a cheap as chips
printing stamp!*

The cost of buying dozens of Christmas cards soon
adds up – so why not get the kids making them
this year? They're sure to be a treat, and each
mini masterpiece will be a true original

Photo: Michelle McInerney MollyMoo.ie

PRINTING AND PAINTING WITH CHILDREN

♡ Make sure you've got the time, space and patience for crafting, and choose a setting that you don't mind getting messy.

♡ Old clothes, and tables or floors covered in newspaper or plastic are a must, especially when using acrylic paints – these are hard to get out of clothes, once dry.

♡ Have baby wipes or paper towels handy for splashes and spills.

♡ Try not to exert too much creative control – let the children experiment with their own choice of colors and styles.

♡ When painting pictures, give them a variety of different brushes so they can test out the different effects.

perfectly fine too. Slice the potatoes in half, and use the piece of the larger potato for the black body and the smaller potato for the white belly. Dab black non-toxic acrylic paint onto the large oval and print onto the card. As this needs to be dry before you apply the next layer, take the time to print as many cards as you need. Once dry, apply white non-toxic acrylic paint to the small oval and print on top of the black oval, towards the base. Add the beak and feet by painting a little orange paint onto a child's fingertips, or apply with a brush, and finish by adding a googly eye in place.

All wrapped up

Combine delicate tissue paper with colorful paper tape or ribbons for gorgeous giftwrap. Add a contrasting colored luggage tag for a beautiful finishing touch

Choose no more than three colors and combine textures, plain, patterns and prints to create the most beautifully wrapped gifts and cards

Ten top tags

designed by Stacey Rogers

Be creative with your gift tags – layer different patterned and textured papers or felt, then cut out different shapes with a hole punch, or add stickers and buttons. Fastening with ribbon is a pretty alternative to attaching your tags with string

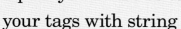

You can buy packs of festive embellishments to make a large collection of coordinating stylish tags

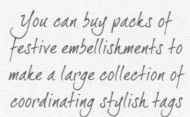

Crafts to Sew

Jolly gingerbread

Looking good enough to eat, these gingerbread decorations are actually made from felt!

If you don't want to cook real cookies this Christmas, you can easily make these felt versions. Simply cut out heart shapes from brown felt fabric, and attach ribbon loops to the top to hang them. Decorate them in any way you like – stitch on simple embroidery like these designs, or attach beads and buttons to look like icing.

Stuffed with love

designed by Joanna Heptinstall

Decorative heart sachets are a popular gift idea, and it's really simple to make your own

Joanna's adorable heart hangers are quite easy to make and a set will be a fabulous gift. They can just be decorative, or you could fill them with some lavender or potpourri, wrapped in a bit of batting, to scent them. Linen tea towels look beautiful, and it will be fun decorating them with buttons and beads.

Give a spare linen tea towel a new lease on life by using it to create these adorable heart sachets, filled with lavender

Photocopy this template at 200% for a full-size heart. Remember that this is only the left half of the shape and the scale is 50%, so your finished template will be much bigger. The dotted line shows the seam allowance for this project, which is the gap you need to leave around the edges when you sew the two fabric hearts together.

Use your heart template to make lots of sachets!

HOW TO MAKE THE HEARTS

Follow steps to make heart sachets as gifts for all your family…

STEP 1

Enlarge the heart template shown at the top of the page, then trace it and transfer it onto a fold in your tea towel. Cut out the heart shape. Hold the fabric firmly and use sharp, strong scissors because tea towel fabric is thick! Once you're done, cut out a second heart the same way. If you want to decorate your hearts then do it now before you sew them up – add pretty buttons or simple embroidered designs.

STEP 2

Next, create a loop from ribbon and pin the raw ends to the top of one of the hearts. Put your two fabric heart shapes right sides together, so that any decoration you've added is facing inwards. Pin, then sew the two hearts together using the seam allowance from the template as a guide, and leave a gap for the stuffing along one straight side. This stitching should hold the ends of the ribbon firmly to produce your hanger. Remove all the pins.

STEP 3

Use small, sharp scissors to snip little V shapes, almost to the sewn line, around the curved edges of the heart. This will give your sachet a smoother shape. Now push the fabric through the gap you left to turn your heart right-side out. Stuff the heart using plain toy stuffing until it's reasonably firm, and add lavender or a few drops of essential oil for a scented finish. Once you're done, carefully sew up the gap by hand.

NOEL HEART SACHETS

Pretty heart sachets make great gifts on their own, but you could adapt the idea to make a festive family banner with our elegant cross stitched Noel set.

This set will make a fab festive display

NOEL HEART SACHET
MATERIAL
☐ 24 count evenweave or 14 count aida, 7x7in (18x18cm) piece for each sachet
☐ Red or white backing fabric, 7x7in (18x18cm) piece for each sachet
☐ Baker's twine or ribbon
☐ Buttons
☐ Stuffing

	DMC	Anchor	Madeira
Cross stitch in two strands			
♥	321	047	0510
Backstitch in one strand			
——	321	047	0510
N O E L outlines			

Try using long stitch or other hand embroidery stitches to create the letters

Red and white is a great Christmas color scheme, but you could add a touch of gold

A HEARTFELT GIFT

Make your heart sachets even more heartfelt with a cross stitched heart in the center of the front – a pair like this will make a great gift for a special couple.

GINGHAM HEART SACHET

MATERIAL

☐ Gingham fabric,
7x7in (18x18cm)
piece for each sachet
☐ Red backing felt,
7x7in (18x18cm)
piece for each sachet
☐ Ribbon
☐ Buttons
☐ Stuffing

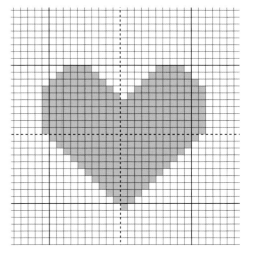

DMC	Anchor	Madeira
Cross stitch in three strands		
White 002		2402
321	047	0510

Stylish stocking

designed by Zoë Patching

A simple chunky running stitch adds a sweet finish to this personalized stocking

Christmas stockings add the finishing touch to your holiday decorations, and they make great gifts, too. Thanks to fusible interfacing – the no-sew solution for adding the contrasting fabrics – you'll be able to rustle up this stylish stocking design in no time, giving you more time to spend with your loved ones. Now that's what we call a perfect Christmas gift!

Photocopy this template at 200% for a full-size stocking or 100% for a small stocking

MAKE THE STOCKING

Step 1: Photocopy the template at 200% for a full-size stocking or at 100% for a small stocking. Cut out the template and pin it onto the fabric, taking care to keep it flat. Place the pins as close as possible to the edge of the template and use lots of them, or the paper will move when you pick up the fabric.

Step 2: Carefully cut out the stocking shape using pinking shears – they will help stop the fabric from fraying, as well as giving your stocking a more interesting edging. Then pin the template down again to the remaining fabric and cut out a second piece. Then cut trims for the toe, heel and top of the stocking from a contrasting piece of patterned fabric, using the main template for guidance.

Step 3: Attach the trims with fusible interfacing, then decorate the front piece with buttons and sequins – follow our photo or create your own design. When you're done, sew around the edges with a chunky running stitch.

SEWING SEQUINS
Secure your thread using backstitch, then position a sequin on your fabric. Starting with your needle on the wrong side of the fabric, push it up through the center of the sequin. Bring your needle back down through the fabric, as close to the edge of your sequin as possible. Repeat the process, moving around the edge of the sequin until it's held firmly in place. Secure your thread or move on to the next sequin if it's less than ¼in (0.5cm) away.

This simple stocking makes a great way to use up any spare fabric scraps you've got lurking in your stash

Top table

designed by Abigail Barker

Impress your guests with a glistening ribbon-trimmed tablecloth for an elegant Christmas meal. We've teamed crisp white tableware with a varied selection of ice-blue satin and organza ribbons, in different widths and textures. You could also make coordinating napkins, and even place cards for a festive special occasion.

This set is so easy to stitch you can make sets for any occasion – simply match your color scheme to the season you're celebrating in, or your own favorite dinner service. We like the idea of bright yellow and crisp white for summer, or deep reds for a romantic Valentine's Day meal.

Complete the ribbon theme with matching name place cards or Christmas menu

PLACE CARDS

Place cards make any meal more of an event, and will really impress your Christmas guests. Cut and fold a small white card, and stick strips of blue card, patterned paper and ribbons across the bottom and right-hand side. You can even weave a few of them together for more interest.

Then punch a hole in the top-left corner. Create a ribbon 'tassel' by first cutting a selection of ribbons, and bunch them together, folded in half. Place them over the punched hole. Wrap the ribbons with a length of coordinating thread, passing the thread ends through the hole. Knot them on the inside of the card to secure.

You could also use this place card design to make up matching dinner party invitations to send to all your guests – that way, you'll get your theme going well before your guests have even arrived!

NAPKIN

Start by cutting a selection of ribbon in a variety of lengths – between 1in (4cm) and 3in (8cm) – and different widths. Fold each ribbon in half and arrange them along the edge of your napkin, pinning them into place.

Using your sewing machine, stitch a straight line over the ends of the ribbons by the folds, as shown. Try cutting the ribbon ends in different ways for a textured finish. After you've sewn the ribbon fringe on, roll up the napkin and tie a bow around it for a pretty finish.

TABLE RUNNER

The table runner is very simple to make – just follow the same instructions as for the napkin and attach the ribbons along the ends of the runner. The only difference is that this time you should make your ribbon lengths longer, to keep everything in proportion.

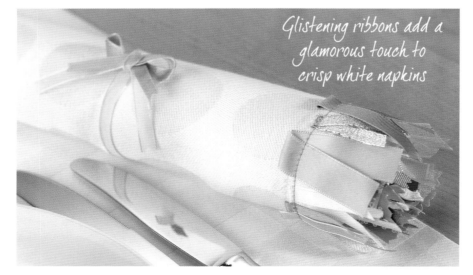

Glistening ribbons add a glamorous touch to crisp white napkins

Crafts with *Paper*

Merry Christmas

comfort & joy

Warm wishes

designed by Angela Poole

Send a beautiful dove card this Christmas, with stitched writing or create the effect in pen. They also make stunning tree decorations and gift tags

Simple shapes look stunning in red and white

MAKE...DOVE DECORATIONS
Stitching on paper is a stylish way of adding a twist to your tree decorations

STEP 1	STEP 2	STEP 3	STEP 4

   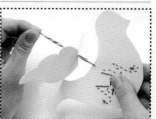

STEP 1
Using the templates on the next page, trace and cut out one body and one wing shape for each dove. Then fold the wing shape in half lengthways.

STEP 2
On the reverse, lightly draw the picture or word you'd like to stitch on your dove. Use a sharp needle to punch holes along the pencil line.

STEP 3
Punch an additional hole at the center top edge of the dove's body and another in the center of the fold on the wing shape. Use six strands for the stitching.

STEP 4
Thread a length of baker's twine through the hole in the dove's body shape. Now thread through the hole in the middle of the wings and pull down to the body.

Hope Joy Love Noel for you

Check the size of your card before you cut out your dove shapes. You may need to slightly change the size of the dove so it fits neatly on the card. Trim the edges with scissors until you have the size you want. To make a single wing for your card, just cut along the dotted line in the centre

Experiment with layering shapes and textures in red and white; add buttons and ribbons for the finishing touches to your cards and decorations

Merry Christmas

JOY

Happy Christmas

Sealed with a kiss

designed by Anna Moore

Get in the Christmas spirit with Anna Moore's stunning cards featuring everyone's favorite festive foliage

Christmas wouldn't be half as cheery if it wasn't for the chance of stealing of a kiss under the mistletoe, and Anna Moore has designed three fabulous cards featuring the festive evergreen.

"I used green metal photo anchors to form the mistletoe that the couple of owls are sat under," says Anna. "I also made an unusual card with a spinning dove suspended in an aperture that's decorated with a festive wreath of mistletoe."

The mantelpiece card is embellished with delicate hand-snipped mistletoe and Anna shows you how to make it in three simple steps.

PAPER PIECE PERFECT OWLS
Paper piece this cute owl couple sitting on a hand-cut branch. Add some festive fun to your card by gluing two green metal photo anchors together to make mistletoe leaves. White brad berries make the perfect finishing touch.

SHOPPING LIST
BASIC CARD KIT, PLUS
☐ White, red, brown, black, light green, dark green, orange, pink & grey card
☐ Assorted digital papers
☐ Mistletoe with Berries dies
☐ Scalloped rectangle & circle dies
☐ Black & white brads
☐ Self-adhesive pearls
☐ Baker's twine
☐ Red embroidery thread
☐ White gel pen
☐ Glue gun
☐ Green metal photo anchors

MAKE AN AMAZING APERTURE CARD
Sketch and snip two basic dove shapes from white card and sandwich a piece of baker's twine between the two pieces. Suspend the dove in the aperture of a card blank, and decorate the aperture with a die-cut mistletoe wreath.

How to snip out a sprig of mistletoe

STEP 1

STEP 2

STEP 3

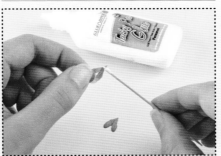

Punch out some small flowers from light green and dark green card. Snip out the tiny individual petals from the flower to make the heart-shaped mistletoe leaves.

Use a toothpick to carefully apply a small amount of glue to each of the mini mistletoe leaves. Layer up the leaves, alternating between light and dark green card.

Decorate the layered sprig of mistletoe using self-adhesive pearls as berries. Use a pair of tweezers to apply the pearl berries to the base of each mistletoe leaf.

Ex-STRAW-ordinary creations

designed by Julie Kirk

10 inspirations for straws

SNIP A STRAW CHRISTMAS TREE

Create a bold Christmas tree using graduating lengths of decorative straw. Simply snip straws to various lengths and line them up on your cards with narrow strips of double-sided tape. This technique makes a good choice if you want to create a big batch of quick, yet memorable festive cards.

date: 25 /12/ 12

CREATE CHRISTMAS CANDY CANES

Even the most basic plain white bendy straw can be made into the sweetest treat for your Christmas cards! Simply cover the back of some red satin ribbon with double-sided tape and carefully wind it around a white straw to decorate it to look like a Christmas candy cane.

TURN SIMPLE STRAWS INTO SNOWFLAKES!

Even ordinary, value-pack straws can be transformed into a pretty textured topper! Snip several lengths of straws and cross them over one another to create a snowflake shape. Secure with glue and layer up with paper circles, buttons and a sentiment to complete!

4

PAPER PIECE A SKIING PENGUIN!

You can't help but smile at this cute penguin on drinking straw skis. Pull the bendy section of the straws into shape to make the skis, then use your favorite papers to make the pattern to paper piece the penguin. Bring your Christmas character to life with a pair of googly eyes!

5

MAKE STRAWS A FANCY FOCAL POINT

Make this clean, no glue, no mess snowflake in minutes! Cross four lengths of striped paper straws over one another, then fix with a decorative brad. Create a simple, sophisticated card background and adhere your straw star in place with double-sided tape.

6

STRING UP SEASONAL STRAW BUNTING

Snip short sections of drinking straws and thread them onto twine for decorative three-dimensional bunting. Use a large, sharp needle to pierce the straws and add small scraps of paper and felt to your bunting for cool textured effects. String up your bunting on tags for the perfect Christmas gift!

7

HAVE SOME FESTIVE FUN!

These drinking straws will provide plenty of fun photo opportunities at Christmas dinner or festive parties! Cut out Santa's beard or Rudolf's nose, then punch a hole in each mouth, thread a straw through and they're ready to use!

MAKE FUN FLAG PLACE SETTINGS

These quick and simple personalized straw flags make ideal decorative place markers for a trendy festive table setting. Glue a strip of patterned paper around a drinking straw then snip a 'V' shape from the end. Add a name with alpha stickers, stamps, or even by hand to personalize your place marker.

HANG UP GORGEOUS HEART DECORATIONS

Glue lengths of straw on top of one another and then snip out simple shapes to create fab three-dimensional hanging decorations. Try gluing your straws together on a non-stick surface rather than gluing it on to card – this will make your decoration double-sided!

GIVE YOUR FAVORITE PHOTOS FABULOUS STRAW FRAMES!

Glue a photo to your scrapbook page and measure the sides, then snip lengths of straw to frame the edges. Straws aren't as chunky as many other embellishments, so your stylish scrapbook pages will still slide into page protectors with ease.

Top tricks for using straws

• It can be tricky to track down decorative patterned paper straws, but smaller online suppliers like The Kids' Table (www.etsy.com/shop/thekidstableshop) are happy to create small custom orders to suit your crafting requirements.

• Standard drinking straws are a really inexpensive way of jazzing up basic cards, and they're available at almost all supermarkets.

• Try wrapping drinking straws in decorative washi tape for impressive one-of-a-kind designs!

Crafts to Crochet

Crochet curtain

designed by Jacqui Harding

Add a natural glamour to your home with this beautiful lace curtain – a luxurious vintage treat

This delicate lace curtain is the perfect crocheted project to add some vintage-inspired charm to your window. Designer Jacqui Harding says: "Images from X-ray crystallography and snowflakes collided when I designed this panel curtain. Mixing two laceweight but very different textured yarns adds another level of interest. Make this in these sophisticated creams for a crisp, vintage old-lace look, or try vivid blue-green-purple colors for a spectacular stained glass feel." The motifs could also be used to create an ethereal scarf or shawl.

FULL MOTIF

Note: make 14 in Angel with 3.5mm hook and 58 in Rialto with 4mm hook (72 total).

Rnd 1 (RS): Loop the yarn around your finger. Working into the loop, ch3, dc, ch2, (2dc into loop, ch2) five times. Join with sl st to top of ch3. Pull on the tail of the loop to close the hole.
Rnd 2 (RS): Sl st along and into 2ch-sp. Ch5, 2dc into same sp. (Into next 2ch-sp: 2dc, ch3, 2dc) 5 times, dc into first 2ch-sp, join with sl st to 3rd ch.
Rnd 3 (RS): Sl st into 3ch-sp, sc into same sp, (ch7, sc into next 3ch-sp) five times, sl st into first sc to join.
Rnd 4 (RS): Sl st into 7ch-sp, ch3, 7dc into same sp, ch3, (8dc into next 7ch-sp, ch3) five times, sl st into 3rd ch. Break yarn and fasten off.

Rnd 5 (RS): On all except the first motif, this is the **joining round**. Fasten the motifs as you go by sl st on the 2nd ch of the ch3 stitches (lobes) in this rnd. Join yarn in any 3ch-sp from rnd 4. Ch3, dc, tr into same sp. Ch3, tr, 3dc into same sp, (sk 3 sts, dc into next 3 sts, sk 2 sts, [3dc, tr, ch3, tr, 3dc] into the next 3ch-sp) five times, sk 3 sts, dc into next 3 sts, sk 2 sts, dc into 3ch-sp, join with sl st to top of ch3. Break yarn and fasten off.

HALF MOTIF

Note: make 4 in Rialto with 4mm hook.

Rnd 1 (WS): Loop the yarn around your finger. Working into the loop, ch5, (2dc into ring, ch2) three times, dc. Pull on the tail of the loop to close the hole.
Rnd 2 (RS): Turn, ch5, 2dc into 2ch-sp, (2dc into next 2ch-sp, ch2, 2dc into same sp) two times, 2dc, ch2, dc into final 5ch-sp.
Rnd 3 (WS): Turn, sc into 2ch-sp, (ch7, sc into next 2ch-sp) 2 times, ch7, sc into final 5ch-sp.

CROCHET CURTAIN

SIZE

☐ Blocked curtain measures approx. 41½inx51in (105x130cm) long

THIS PROJECT WAS STITCHED USING

☐ Debbie Bliss Rialto Lace (Lace weight; 100% merino; 426yds /390m per 1¾oz/50g ball) Shade 12; 3 x 1¾oz/50g balls
☐ Debbie Bliss Angel (Lace weight; 76% mohair, 24% silk; 219yds /200m per ⅞oz/25g ball) Shade 5; 2 x ⅞oz/25g balls
☐ Matching polyester or silk sewing thread (optional)

HOOKS & ACCESSORIES

☐ 4mm (UK 8/US 6) crochet hook
☐ 3.5mm (UK9/US 4/E) crochet hook
☐ Tapestry needle

GAUGE

☐ A full motif measures approx 6¾in (17cm) point to point when blocked, using a 4mm hook for motifs made in Rialto and a 3.5mm hook for motifs made in Angel

Turn to page 51 for your blocking diagram and chart

Hang your curtain against a natural source of light so you can see the lacy details of the crochet shapes clearly

THE KNITTER
This project was originally featured in *The Knitter*.

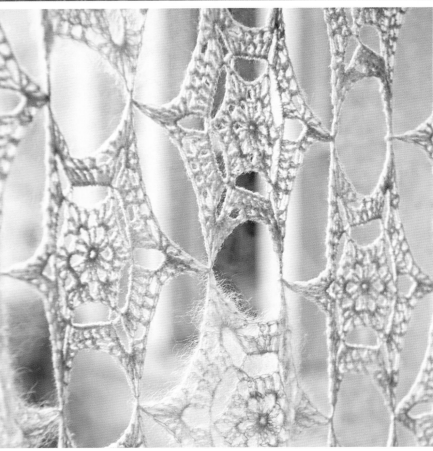

Rnd 4 (RS): Turn, ch6 (8dc into 7ch-sp, ch3) three times, dc into sc. Break yarn.

Rnd 5 (RS): Rejoin yarn at left side into 3ch-sp with RS facing. Ch6, sl st join to motif, ch1, tr, 3dc into same sp. Sk 3 sts, dc into top of next 3 sts. Sk 2 sts, (3dc, tr, ch3*, tr, 3dc into 3ch-sp. Sk 3 sts, dc into next 3sts, sk 2 sts) two times, 3dc, tr, ch3*, tr into 6ch-sp. Break yarn and fasten off.
* Join to adjoining motif by sl st at 2nd ch.

CURTAIN TOP EDGING

Work using Rialto. You will need both hook sizes for this section.

Tip: Fsc is usually worked through two loops, but I found it much easier to work through one, and I like the looped effect that it gives.
For extra strength, use matching silk or polyester sewing thread and Rialto held double on Rows 2 to 5.

Row 1 (RS): With RS facing and 4mm hook, join yarn at the top right hand side. Connect the yarn through the top right lobe of the motif. *Fsc 12, sl st to connection point between the two motifs. Along the top of the half motif, work 3 sc in each ch or dc sp to centre (12 sc total), repeat on other side, sl st to join at connection point. Repeat from * to end of last half motif, fsc 12. Sl st the last fsc to lobe.

Row 2: Switch to 3.5mm hook. Ch3, turn, dc into each st across.

Row 3: ch3, turn, dc into same st, going under all three strands into the space below, * ch2, sk next two sts, tr as before into next three sts, repeat from * to last three sts, ch2, 2dc into last st.

Row 4: Ch3, turn, *2 dc into 2ch-sp, dc into top of next three sts, repeat from * to end.

Row 5: Ch2 turn, sc into each st across. Break yarn and fasten off.

BOTTOM EDGING

Work using Angel and 4mm hook.

With RS facing, turn the curtain upside down, so the bottom is at the top! With 4mm hook, attach the Angel at the right-hand lobe. Make sure you attach at the 1st point of the bottom – not the side point.

Row 1 (RS): Ch3, 1dc into 1st st, *tr into each of next nine sts, de into next st (which is the st at the left edge of this motif), 2dc into 3ch-sp (which is the starting edge of the next motif). **Dc into next seven sts, sc into next 3 sts, 2 sc into 3ch-sp, sc across to next 3ch-sp, 2sc into space, sc into next three sts, dc in each st to next motif, 2dc into the first 3ch-sp of this motif. Rep from * across, ending at **

Row 2: Turn, Ch4, tr into next nine st, *(sk 1 st, tr into next st) two times. (sk 1 st, dc into next st) three times, dc into next three st. sk 1 st, dc. Sc into next st, 2 sc into next two st (top of the lobe), sc. Sk 1 st, dc into next five sts, sk 1 st, dc. Sc into next two sts, 2sc into next two sts (top of lobe), sc. (Sk 1 st, dc) two times. 4dc, (sk 1 st, dc) two times, sk 1 st, tr, sk 1 st, tr into next eight sts. Repeat from * to end.

Row 3: Turn, Work 1 sc into each st. At the lobe points, work three sc into 1 st. Fasten off, and weave in all ends.

ALTERNATE BOTTOM EDGING

If you prefer a straight edge at the bottom, this can be achieved by replacing the four bottom motifs with half motifs. This will make the curtain approximately 2⅜in (6cm) shorter. Finish the bottom edge, using Angel and a 4mm hook, by two rows of tr followed by 1 row of sc.

FINISHING

Wet block the piece (using blocking wires will make this much easier), pinning out the connections at the sides and using spray starch if desired.

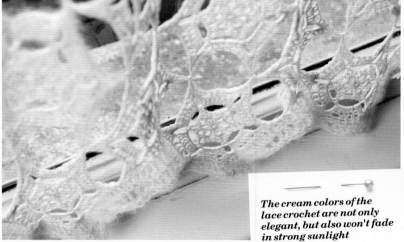

The cream colors of the lace crochet are not only elegant, but also won't fade in strong sunlight

NOTES

The curtain is made of 76 motifs; 14 are full motifs made in Angel, 58 are full motifs made in Rialto and four are half motifs made in Rialto. They are joined together as you complete the last round of each motif; please refer to the schematic diagram for the layout. The curtain is then finished off by adding two different borders, one to the top of the curtain using Rialto and another to the bottom of the curtain using Angel.

Changing the length of the curtain

A shorter length can be achieved by reducing the number of rows of motifs in the schematic diagram, shown above. A longer curtain can be achieved by adding extra rows of motifs and/or extra rows of dtr's on the finishing until you achieve your desired length. However, please be aware that you may require extra balls of yarn to do this.

SPECIAL ABBREVIATIONS

rnd: round
st: stitch
ch: chain stitch
sl st: slip stitch
dc: Double crochet stitch
tr: Treble or Triple stitch
sk: skip
sp: space
ch-sp: chain space
yrh: yarn round hook
fsc: foundation single crochet stitch – ch 2, insert hook into loop of 2nd ch, pull yarn though, yrh, pull yarn through both loops.* Insert hook into front loop of base of sc just made, yrh, pull up loop, yrh, pull through both stitches. Repeat from *

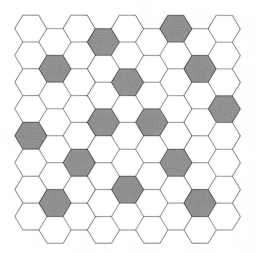

BLOCKING DIAGRAM

Schematic and joining diagram: without top and bottom border, shaded hexagons represent Angel motifs

KEY

•	Slip stitch
O	Chain
✕	Single crochet
⊢	Double crochet
⊬	Treble or Triple crochet

CHART

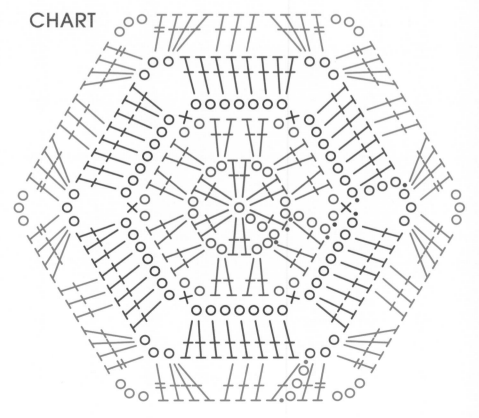

Bag charm

designed by Cara Medus

Cara's bag charm adds festive cheer to any type of bag, but don't let it stop there… why not decorate your boots, hats and lapels, too? Or hang one in the car. They're perfect for stocking stuffers too!

THIS PROJECT WAS STITCHED USING

Wendy, Supreme Luxury Cotton sport weight (US8) (100% cotton, 3½oz/100g, 220yds/201m) 1 ball of each: Beet (1949) and White (1820)

HOOKS & ACCESSORIES

A 5mm crochet hook
Ribbon
Split ring
Buttons and beads (optional)

MEASUREMENTS

Motif 1 measures 4¾in (12cm) diameter using 5mm hook

MOTIF 1

With Beet, ch 6 and join with a ss into a ring.

Round 1 Ch 1, 10 sc into the ring, slst to the first ch to join.

Round 2 Ch 3, 2 sc tog into first st, ch 1 (3 sc tog into next st, ch 1) 9 times, slst to 3rd ch at beg of round to join, turn.

Round 3 Ch 1, (sc in next ch 1 sp, ch 2) 10 times, slst to ch 1 at beg of round, turn.

Round 4 Ch 3, into first 2-ch sp work the following: 1 dc, ch 1, 2 dc, ch 1. *Into next 2-ch sp work the following: (2 dc, 1 ch) twice. Rep from * another 8 times, ss to 3rd ch at beg of round to join.

Round 5 Slst into first 1-ch sp. Ch 3, into 1st 1-ch sp work the following: 2 dc, ch 2, 3 dc, ch 2. *Skip next 1-ch sp, and into the next 1-ch sp work the following: (3 dc, ch 2) twice. Rep from * another 8 times, slst to 3rd ch at the beg of the round to join.

Round 6 Slst over first 2 tr of previous round and slst into 1st 2-ch sp. Ch 3, 7 dc into same 2-ch sp, ch 2. *Skip next 2-ch sp, and into the next 2-ch sp work the following: 8 dc, ch 2. Rep from * another 8 times, slst to 3rd ch at beg of round to join. Fasten off.

Round 7 With White, ss into one of the 2-ch sp of the previous round. Ch 1, *sc into each of the 8 dc of the previous round, sc into the next 2-ch sp, ch 1. Now work towards the centre of the motif as follows: sc into the 2-ch sp of round 5, ch 1, sc into the 1-ch sp of round 4, ch 1, sc into the dc of round 3, ch 1. Now work towards the edge of the motif in the same ch sps as follows: sc into the 1-ch sp of round 4, ch 1, sc into the 2-ch sp of round 5, ch 1, sc into the 2-ch sp of round 6. Rep from * another 9 times, ss to the first ch of the round to join. Fasten off.

MOTIF 2

With White, Ch 4 and slst to join into a ring.

Round 1 Ch 1, 6 sc into ring, slst to the first ch of the round to join. [6 sts]

Round 2 Ch 1, 2 sc into each sc of the previous round, slst to the first ch of the round to join. [12 sts]

Round 3 Ch 3, dc in the st at the base of the ch, ch 3. *Skip 1 st, 2 dc tog in next st, ch 3. Rep from * another 4 times, slst to 3rd ch at the beg of the round to join.

Round 4 *Ch 3, 3 dc tog in st at base of ch, ch 3, slst into same st, 3 sc in 3-ch sp of previous round, slst in next st. Rep from * another 5 times.

Round 5 Slst into first 3 ch of previous round. *Ch 6, slst into st at base of ch, ch 6, skip 1 sc of previous round and sc into next sc, ch 6, slst into top of 3 dc tog of previous round. Rep from * another 5 times. Fasten off.

MOTIF 3

With Beet, ch 8 and ss to the first ch to join into a ring.

Round 1 Ch 1, 12 sc into the ring, ss to the first ch to join.

Round 2 *Ch 6, skip next st, sc in next. Rep from * another 5 times, ss into first 6-ch sp to finish.

Fasten off.

FINISHING

Weave in all ends. Attach a loop of ribbon to the back of each motif, varying the length of the ribbon so that the motifs are layered over the center of each other. Thread alternating beads and buttons onto another piece of ribbon and fold over to form a small loop on the other end. Put all loops of ribbon on a split ring.

ABBREVIATIONS

2 dc tog 2 double crochet together as follows: *yrh and insert into next st, yrh and draw yarn through st. Yrh and draw through first 2 loops on hook. Rep from * once more. Yrh and draw yarn through all the loops on hook.
Where the pattern indicates to work '2 dc tog in next st', work all this in the one stitch without moving on to the next.

3 dc tog as 2 dc tog, but rep from * three times in total, yrh and draw through all loops on hook.

Step-by-Step Single Crochet

STEP 1	STEP 2	STEP 3

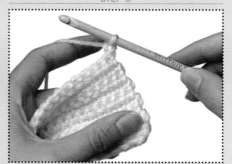

Insert the hook under the top two loops of the first stitch on the previous row.

Wind the yarn around the hook and pull it through the stitch, leaving two loops on your crochet hook.

Yarn round hook again, then pull the yarn through both loops. You'll have one loop left on your hook ready to do the next stitch.

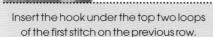

Crafts to Cross Stitch

Have a Crafty Christmas!

Designer Helen Philipps invites us into her gorgeous home and talks about how she prepares for the festive season

Helen Philipps

Whether you're an experienced crafter, or just enjoy adding a personal touch to everyday objects around your home, Christmas is the perfect time of year to express your creativity and enthusiasm, producing cards, gifts and festive decorations. Cross stitch designer Helen Philipps, shares her expert tips on planning for a crafty Christmas at home.

Q *What's your home like at Christmas?*

A I make my home cozy, with lamps, candles, firelight, quilts and cushions – lots of nice festive things but not too cluttered, to keep it feeling calm. Sometimes I put groups of things together that are not strictly Christmassy but still give that feel – like using ruby red glasses for tea lights, and cozy red and white quilts on the sofa.

Gorgeous garlands Even simple shapes in festive colors look fantastic when strung together in garlands

Simply stylish Helen's felt heart were embroidered with Shaker-style festive motifs

Q *When do you begin decorating your home for Christmas, and which area of the house do you start with?*

A Christmas just sort of creeps up on me! On shopping trips I look out for current Christmas products such as jars of red and white striped sweets, pretty cookie tins or glass jars, which then become part of my decorations. I start with decorating the kitchen, where the first cards begin to collect, and I love having seasonal candles on the table and candle bridge lights in the windows. In other rooms I get out favorite Christmas samplers. Sometimes I hang them on a wall in place of another picture temporarily, and sometimes I prop them up on a shelf or mantelpiece. I usually put the tree up during the second week of December.

Q *How do you go about planning your decorations? Do you make new ones each year, and do you have old favorites?*

A I don't really plan the decorations – I just build on what I have and tie it in with the current theme of the house. Quilts are taken out and placed on the sofas, and sometimes I get an idea for something to make like an appliqué stocking or a tree decoration, but it's very spontaneous! I use things I've made for books and magazines, and little toys like my gingerbread men and jingle bell bunny form part of my decorations. I have a lot of red and white tree decorations that I keep using, and I've made some felt hearts with embroidery, which were inspired by Shaker designs. Last year I made another one to add to the set – a red and white toadstool.

Toasty toes Turn to page 66 to discover how to make baby slippers like these

Welcome home Helen's handmade gingerbread men make a regular appearance at Christmas, along with cross stitched door hangers

Snow is falling... Helen's Christmas samplers bring the festive spirit into her home

Q *If someone wants to recreate this festive look, where should they start?*

A This is a hard question to answer, as my home has just evolved. I gradually bought pale furniture, painted dark furniture, and made quilts and cushions. Into that mix each year I add whatever Christmas decorations I have collected or made – it's not really a thought-out style, just my own idea of Christmas at home!

Jingle bells This friendly festive bunny is another favorite decoration

Q *What about color – how does a color scheme influence your designs?*

A I love the red and white Nordic style, and combined with a bit of green that's my favorite Christmas look at the moment. It also fits in with my cream sofas and painted furniture. Pretty cards, painted wooden ornaments and vintage china look lovely together on the dresser, surrounded by strings of lights, berries or rag garlands.

Q *What inspires your cross stitch creations?*

A My work is inspired by anything and everything I see! I'm always looking for things of interest – color combinations, pattern, texture and things that I love. I absorb all these different things and then they come out in my work eventually. I love to look at all kinds of art and design, magazines, interiors, shops, high street fashion, and all kinds of decorative products, whether they're vintage or brand new... absolutely everything interests me visually!

Q *What are your favorite materials to work with, and which are easiest to work with for festive decorations?*

A For Christmas decorations I would suggest using felt, beads, embroidery, patchwork, cross stitch, simple appliqué and papercraft. I also love to sew any interesting buttons on to my cross stitch designs, embroidery and quilts, and I glue them on to papercraft projects too.

Q *What can people do at home to have a beautiful and thrifty Christmas?*

A Use fabric you already have for making quilts, cushions and small padded heart and bird decorations, or look in thrift shops for fabric or clothing that can be cut up. Save colored selvedge and use as ribbon in your projects, and look for bundles of ribbon and braid in thrift shops. Make paper decorations from old book pages – cut out shapes with a decorative punch and string together, or use colored magazine pages for colorful garlands.

Q *You're famous for your intricate samplers and cross stitch designs. Do you cross stitch festive cards and samplers?*

A Each year I design cross stitch Christmas samplers for magazines so I usually do create a new festive sampler (though not always during the festive season, as the designs have to be submitted well in advance!). Sometimes I've stitched a Christmas sampler especially for my home, and later it has been used in a book or magazine. If I feel inspired I like to make what's in my head! I don't usually cross stitch my own Christmas cards these days, as I make so many for magazine projects, but I do make small gifts for family and friends – last year it was stitched sweetie bags to put small gifts in, made of red and white striped fabric with rubber-stamped tags tied with different red or white ribbon.

HOW TO GET SIMPLE CHRISTMAS STYLE

☐ Collect lots of things you could use to make decorations over the year – cans and jam jars, scraps of tissue paper, fabric, ribbon and broken beads. Then at Christmas see what you can make!

☐ Cover a can with bright paper, glue on a festive motif and fill it with candy canes.

☐ Tie ribbon round a jar and add a tea light, or add a bunch of festive greenery and berries.

☐ Make stuffed hanging hearts with scraps of fabric and decorate with vintage buttons. It's surprising how ideas occur to you if you have lots of crafty materials to play with!

Home sweet home

designed by Helen Philipps

Add traditional motifs to fabric by stitching or painting, then include roofs and doors to create miniature houses

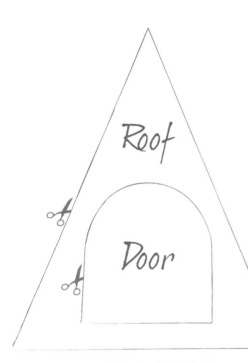

Use this simple template to make the roof and door for your little house decorations.

If you enjoy cross stitch you can follow these charts to create the designs; if not, you can paint your motifs in the middle of a piece of plain fabric. Then trim it to 3½x4¾in (9x12cm), with the top of your motif about 1in (3cm) from the top edge.

Trace the roof template (below left) onto a patterned piece of fabric and cut out ⅜in (1cm) beyond the traced shape. With the right sides in, stitch the bottom of the roof to the top of your stitched/painted fabric. Cut some felt to the same shape for the back.

Trace and cut out the door shape, leaving ⅜in (1cm) of excess fabric along the bottom edge only. Attach to the bottom of your house using fabric glue or running stitch. Sew on a button and attach some ribbon along the roof edge.

With right sides in, sew your front and back pieces together, sandwiching a baker's twine loop at the top and leaving an opening for turning. Turn, fill with stuffing and slip stitch it closed.

Great for decorating your tree

DMC	Anchor	Maderia
Cross stitch in two strands		
♥ 349	046	0212
★ 702	226	1306
0 3865	926	2403
Backstitch in two strands		
—— 702	226	1306
snowflakes		
Backstitch in one strand		
—— 349	046	0212
heart		
French knots in one strand		
● 702	226	1306
snowflakes		

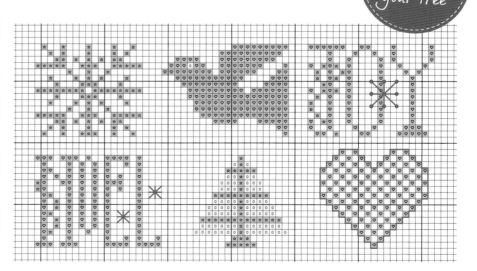

You can also paint or stitch extra motifs on scraps of fabric to make matching gift tags and place cards

Christmas chic

designed by Anette Eriksson

A mini cushion like this heart is a great quick make that looks so pretty hung up

Make a beautiful handmade cushion and decorate it with buttons or brooches, embroidery or a cross stitch design…

Of all the things that turn a house into a home, cushions are right at the top of the list, with their cozy invitation to get comfortable. And it's just the same at Christmas – a handmade, festive cushion is just the thing to make your family and your guests feel welcome.

Follow our simple step-by-step guides on the following pages to make this stylish pair of cushions – one square and one little heart. You can decorate the front with any design you like, but if you'd like to make cushions that match ours, just use the easy-to-follow charts to cross stitch these pretty mistletoe designs on linen fabric.

MAKE A... PIPED CUSHION

STEP 1	STEP 2	STEP 3

To make your piping cord, you'll need a 2x60in (5x150cm) strip of fabric. Cut your strips diagonally across the grain of your fabric. Sew together a few shorter pieces if necessary. Wrap your strip around a thin piping cord and pin it in place.	Switch to a machine zipper foot and machine sew up to the edge of the piping cord. Tack your fabric-covered cord in place around the outside edge of your cushion front. You can cut notches in the excess fabric at the corners.	Place your backing fabric over the cushion front and pin. Still using a zipper foot, machine sew right up to the piping edge. Leave an opening for turning. Turn, fill with stuffing and slip stitch closed.

This stunning cushion is a cozy way to welcome Christmas visitors into your home

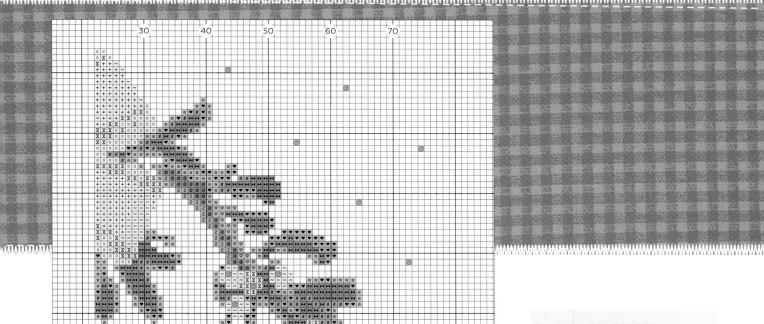

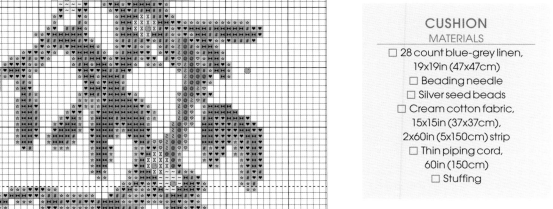

CUSHION
MATERIALS
☐ 28 count blue-grey linen,
19x19in (47x47cm)
☐ Beading needle
☐ Silver seed beads
☐ Cream cotton fabric,
15x15in (37x37cm),
2x60in (5x150cm) strip
☐ Thin piping cord,
60in (150cm)
☐ Stuffing

	DMC	Anchor	Madeira
Cross stitch in three strands			
+	Ecru	390	2404
@	610	889	2106
2	611	898	2107
♡	612	832	2108
⋈	934	862	1506
#	935	861	1505
♥	936	846	1507
☆	937	268	1504
✕	3033	391	1908
~	3865	387	2403
0	3866	926	1901
Attach beads with cotton			

MAKE A... HEART SACHET
Two easy steps to a polished, professional finish

STEP 1

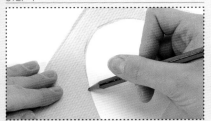

Cut a basic heart template out of card. Use the template to trace and cut out your piece of stitching (or other front fabric) and a piece of backing fabric.

STEP 2

With right sides facing, sew your heart shapes together, sandwiching a ribbon in between. Leave a turning gap. Turn right way out, stuff and slip stitch closed.

HEART SACHET
MATERIAL
- ☐ 28 count blue-grey linen, 10x12in (25x30cm)
- ☐ Cream cotton fabric, 6¾x9½in (17x24cm)
- ☐ Twine
- ☐ Mother-of-pearl button
- ☐ Stuffing

	DMC	Anchor	Madeira
Cross stitch in three strands			
#	935	861	1505
☆	937	268	1504
X	3033	391	1908
~	3865	387	2403

A cord and a hand-sewn button turn this little sachet into a decoration you'll love to hang up every Christmas

Festive feet

designed by Maria Diaz

BABY BOOTIES
MATERIALS

- ☐ 14 count waste canvas, two 2⅜x2⅜in (6x6cm) pieces
- ☐ Thick red felt
- ☐ Wooden buttons

STEP 1

Use waste canvas to stitch your designs onto felt. Cut out two felt pieces of each. Center your stitching on the upper pieces. Sew one upper piece to the front of a sole piece. Bring your needle from the top to the bottom, then again from the top to the bottom, creating loops around the join.

STEP 2

Once you've attached the upper piece to the sole, attach the back piece to the other side of the sole. The back piece should overlap the upper piece slightly. Add a wooden button to both sides, at the point where the pieces overlap.

Make these tiny felt slippers for the youngest in your family – you can decorate them with a seasonal button, or add some cross stitch or embroidery

TEMPLATES

Use these shapes to create the pieces for your booties

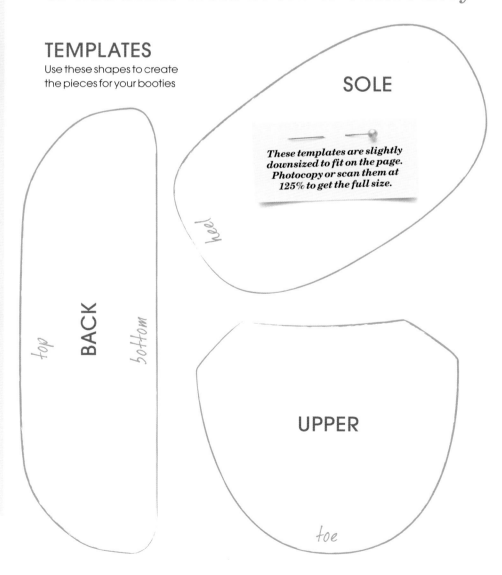

SOLE

These templates are slightly downsized to fit on the page. Photocopy or scan them at 125% to get the full size.

heel

BACK

top

bottom

UPPER

toe

Sweet slippers that will keep tiny feet cozy all year round. Embellish with buttons, embroider initials or cross stitch our festive chart.

	DMC	Anchor	Madeira
Cross stitch in three strands			
~	B5200	001	2401
S	434	310	2009
▲	436	363	2011
♥	666	046	0210
0	738	361	2013
⋈	3371	382	2004
Ǝ	DMC Light Effects E3852		
Backstitch in one strand			
—	666	046	0210
noses			
—	3371	382	2004
mouths			

Decorative letters

designed by Felicity Hall

This alphabet is perfect for festive personalizing. If you don't fancy cross stitch you can copy the letters in fabric pens, or you could print them instead

FESTIVE LETTERS

MATERIALS
☐ 28 count rustic linen, 4¾x4¾in (12x12cm) piece for each letter

DMC	Anchor	Madeira
Cross stitch in three strands		
★ 505	211	1206
△ 666	046	0210
○ 702	226	1306
♥ 777	044	0601

PRINT ONTO FABRIC
Instead of sewing the letters onto fabric, you can buy special paper that you can use in an ordinary inkjet printer to transfer any design onto material. Simply draw out a stylish alphabet and scan it, or design one straight onto your computer. Then you can print it onto the transfer paper, and iron or sew it onto your plain backing fabric.

STITCH IT ON AIDA
If you're a keen stitcher you can work on 14 count rustic aida.

It's a gift Put an initial on a frayed patch of fabric, stick it onto a brown tag, then swap the string for twine to complete the rustic look

From the heart Use a running stitch to attach your letter to an existing heart sachet or make your own

Christmas cards Back your letter with white paper, then attach it to a card using 3D foam pads for a raised effect

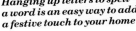
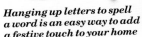

Hanging up letters to spell a word is an easy way to add a festive touch to your home

Try spelling fun, festive words such as CHRISTMAS, JOY, NOEL and PEACE to welcome your guests

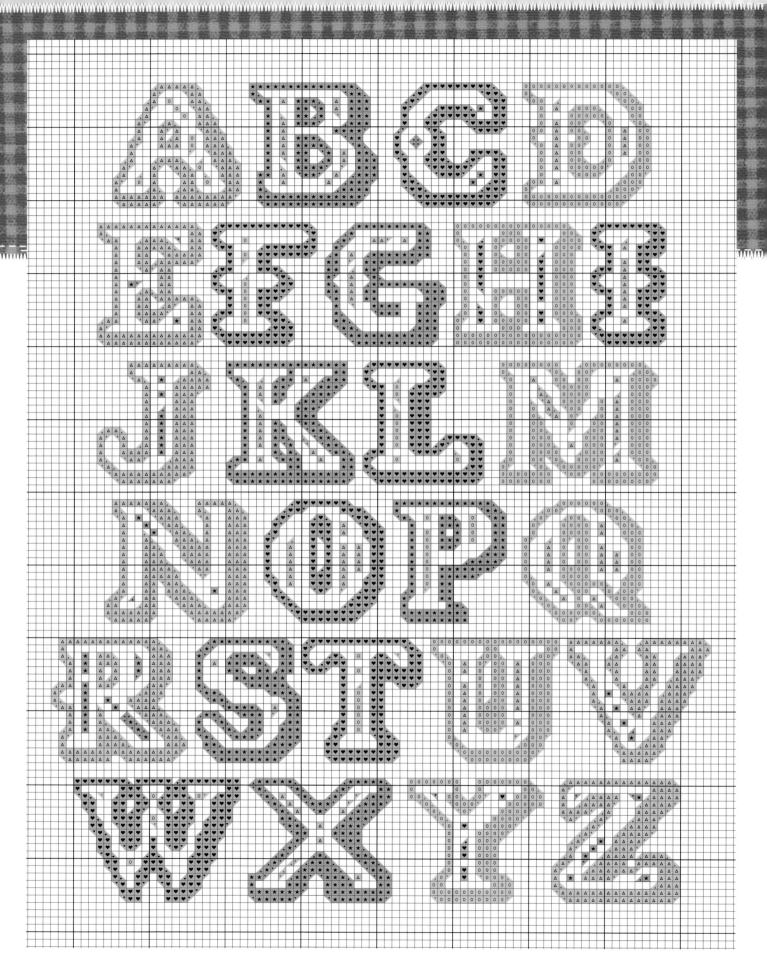

Little rascals!

designed by Kerry Morgan

These cute handmade characters are easy to make and perfect as gifts for kids – create the picture with embroidery, fabric paint, or print onto fabric printer sheets…

Monsters love hanging onto your keys!

MAKE A...PADDED KEYRING

Create a little monster and get him all shaped up to look after your keys in scary style!

STEP 1

Draw a sewing line on the reverse of your character design, following the shape of the monster. Make the shape as fluid as possible, or it will be difficult to sew accurately.

STEP 2

Cut out your monster plus a felt piece ⅜in (1cm) larger than your sewing line. With right sides facing, pin in place, sandwiching a ribbon loop at the top. Sew, leaving an opening.

STEP 3

Turn right sides out. Don't worry if it takes a few tries to get the shape just right. Fill with stuffing and slip stitch the opening closed. Attach your keyring around the ribbon loop.

Get your kids to draw their own monsters on fabric and then turn their creations into fun gifts for cousins or friends

Felt is a perfect fabric for book covers – it's flexible and strong, and there's a huge choice of bright colors

Create a monster cover to keep your favorite book safe

MAKE A...FELT BOOK COVER

Protect a notebook or exercise book with a cover starring a friendly monster guardian

STEP 1

Cut a piece of felt to measure 9x17¼in (22.5x44cm). If you're not using an 5¼"x8¼" notebook, you will need to adjust the size to suit. Trim your monster patch to measure 4x5in (10x12.5cm). Fray the edge of your patch.

STEP 2

Lay your piece of felt on a flat surface. Position your patch in place so the right-hand edge is 3½in (9cm) from the right-hand edge of the felt. Stitch your patch in place using a brightly colored running stitch.

STEP 3

Make a 2⅜in (6cm) fold toward the reverse on both edges and pin in place. Check your book fits snugly. Using a zig zag stitch or a running stitch, sew along the top and bottom edges. Now pop in your book!

Felt turns a frame from functional into funky!

MAKE A...FELT FRAME
When a traditional frame just won't suit, go for a funky felt version

STEP 1
Cut an oval from a piece of turquoise felt. On the reverse side, sketch and cut out a scalloped edge. Now cut an oval aperture from the center, leaving a frame as wide as you like to suit the size of design you're framing.

STEP 2
Now cut an oval aperture in the center of a piece of orange felt, just slightly smaller than the turquoise felt. Then cut scallops around the outside of your orange felt, just slightly larger than the scallops on your turquoise felt.

STEP 3
Back your monster with iron-on interfacing. Pin in place behind your felt pieces. Add contrasting straight stitches around the inside edge of the frame. Add running stitch around the outside edge. Finish with a ribbon loop.

MAKE A...PENCIL CASE
Using Velcro instead of a zip makes this pencil case super quick

STEP 1

Cut a piece of fabric to measure 5¼x7⅞in (13x20cm). Back with iron-on interfacing. Cut three more pieces of patterned fabric to the same size.

STEP 2

With right sides facing, sew one patterned piece and your monster together along the top edge only. Repeat with the other two pieces.

STEP 3

With right sides together, line up both sewn pieces so the joins line up. Sew all the way around, leaving an opening for turning on the lining side.

STEP 4

Turn right side out and slip stitch the opening closed. Push the lining inside. Press the folds flat. Add Velcro or metal fasteners to finish.

Crayons need a colorful monster to look after them!

Crafts to Knit

Debbie Bliss

At home with...
Debbie Bliss

Debbie's designs are so stylish and her Christmas décor is too. Here is how she styles her festive home.

WHERE WILL YOU SPEND CHRISTMAS – WHO WITH, AND WHY? At home as always; even though my children are in their twenties they still like to have Christmas day at home. I will celebrate it with my husband, two children and mother-in-law, plus my nephew and his wife and two children; I'm sure there will be more round the table at some point too. We'll eat, drink, be merry and watch lots of TV.

WHAT'S YOUR BEST EVER CHRISTMAS MEMORY? When the children were young my late father-in-law would ring a bell and race with the children to the window. Then he would explain that they had just missed seeing Santa and his sleigh disappear behind a roof.

WHAT IS YOUR FAVORITE CHRISTMAS RITUAL? On Christmas Eve, watching the King's College carols on TV, eating smoked salmon on brown bread and drinking pink Prosecco.

DO YOU HAVE A FAVORITE FESTIVE COLOR OR THEME? It changes every year, but I always get out my blue flocked Madonna, colored lights and Diptyque Feu de Bois candle.

WHAT IS YOUR EASIEST FESTIVE CRAFT? Pom poms, which I can hang on the tree or string over the mirror. I have so much leftover yarn that it's a great way to use up, and something children can help to make.

WHAT IS THE MOST APPRECIATED GIFT YOU'VE MADE? Anything I ever gave my mother was greeted with great delight. When I first left art college I made knitted plants, and she was proud of her collection!

WHAT IS YOUR FAVORITE PLACE TO SHOP FOR CHRISTMAS GIFTS? Online, because work always gets in the way of shopping in the real world.

THE KNITTER'S YEAR
by Debbie Bliss,
published by Quadrille

Pom Poms are a great way to use up left over yarn, says Debbie. Hang them over mirrors or almost anywhere!

The right scent creates a special atmosphere Debbie loves the aroma of Diptyque's Feu de Bois candles in her home at Christmas

Knitted plants make a unique gift! Debbie made some for her mom back in her college days...

Party shrug

designed by Debbie Bliss

SHORT SHRUG
THIS PROJECT
WAS STITCHED USING

☐ Debbie Bliss Party Angel
(Lace weight; 72% superkid
mohair, 24% silk, 4% metalized
polyester; 219yds/200m,
⅞oz/25g balls)

NEEDLES

☐ 1 pair 3.25mm (UK 10/US 3)
knitting needles
☐ 1 pair 4mm (UK 8/US 6)
knitting needles
☐ 1 pair 4.5mm (UK 7/US 7)
knitting needles

GAUGE

☐ 22 sts and 30 rows to
4in (10cm) over st st using
4mm needles

Knit this stunning shrug as a gift for someone special this Christmas

LEFT SLEEVE

With 4mm needles, cast on 58 (58:62:
62:66:66:70:70:74:74) sts.
Rib row 1: K2, (P2, K2) to end.
Rib row 2: P2, (K2, P2) to end.
Rep the last 2 rows 14 times more.

Change to 3.25mm needles.
Work a further 30 rows in rib.

Change to 4mm needles.
Beg with a K row, work in st st until
sleeve measures 22½in (57cm) from
cast-on edge, ending with a P row **.
Next row: K to last 4 sts, K2tog, K2.
Next row: P to end.
Rep the last 2 rows until 29 (29:31:31:33:
33:35:35:37:37) sts rem.
Work a further 10 (12:14:16:18:20:22:24:
26:28) rows.
Cast off.

RIGHT SLEEVE

Work as given for Left Sleeve to **.
Next row: K2, skpo, K to end.
Next row: P to end.
Rep the last 2 rows until 29 (29:31:31:33:
33:35:35:37:37) sts rem.
Work a further 10 (12:14:16:18:20:22:24:
26:28) rows.
Cast off.

**LEFT FRONT BORDER
AND COLLAR**

With right side of left sleeve facing and
4mm needles, pick up and knit 10 (12:14:
16:18:20:22:24:26:28) sts across back
neck, then 56 (58:60:62:64:66:68:70:72:
74) sts along raglan edge.
66 (70:74:78:82:86:90:94:98:102) sts.

Row 1: P2, (K2, P2) to end.
This row sets the rib.
Next 2 rows: Rib 10 (10:14:14:18:18:22:
22:26:26), turn, rib to end.
Next 2 rows: Rib 14 (14:18:18:22:22:26:
26:30:30), turn, rib to end.
Next 2 rows: Rib 18 (18:22:22:26:26:
30:30:34:34), turn, rib to end.
Next 2 rows: Rib 22 (22:26:26:30:30:
34:34:38:38), turn, rib to end.

Cont in this way, working 4 extra sts on
every right side row until all 66 (70:74:
78:82:86:90:94:98:102) sts have been
taken into work, ending with a wrong
side row.
Rib 2 rows.
Inc row: K2, (P2, K1, M1, K1) to last 4
sts, P2, K2.

Change to 4.5mm needles.
Next row: P2, (K2, P3) to last 4 sts, K2,
P2.
Next row: K2, (P2, K3) to last 4 sts, P2,
K2.
Rib a further 17 rows across all sts.
Cast off loosely in rib.

**RIGHT FRONT BORDER
AND COLLAR**

With right side of right sleeve facing and
4mm needles, pick up and knit 56 (58:
60:62:64:66:68:70:72:74) sts along
raglan edge, then 10(12:14:16:18:20:22:
24:26:28) sts across back neck.
66 (70:74:78:82:86:90:94:98:102) sts.
Row 1: P2, (K2, P2) to end.
Row 2: K2, (P2, K2) to end.
These 2 rows set the rib.
Next 2 rows: Rib 10 (10:14:14:18:18:22:

22:26:26), turn, rib to end.
Next 2 rows: Rib 14 (14:18:18:22:22:26:
26:30:30), turn, rib to end.
Next 2 rows: Rib 18 (18:22:22:26:26:
30:30:34:34), turn, rib to end.
Next 2 rows: Rib 22 (22:26:26:30:30:
34:34:38:38), turn, rib to end.

Cont in this way working 4 extra sts on
every right side row until all the sts have
been worked, ending with a right side
row.
Work 1 row.
Inc row: K2, (P2, K1, M1, K1) to last 4
sts, P2, K2.

Change to 4.5mm needles.
Next row: P2, (K2, P3) to last 4 sts, K2,
P2.
Next row: K2, (P2, K3) to last 4 sts, P2,
K2.
Rib a further 17 rows across all sts.
Cast off loosely in rib.

LOWER BACK BORDER

Join back and collar seam.
Join sleeve seam from cast-on edge to
beg of raglan shaping.
With right side facing and 4mm needles,
pick up and knit 86 (90:94:98:102:106:
110:114:118:122) sts along row ends.
Row 1: P2, (K2, P2) to end.
Row 2: K2, (P2, K2) to end.
Rep the last 2 rows 10 times more and
the first row again.
Cast off in rib.

FINISHING

Join row ends of back border to row ends
of collar to form side seams.

You'll sparkle in this beautiful shrug, made with Debbie Bliss Party Angel yarn, which has a subtle shimmer

BLOCKING DIAGRAM

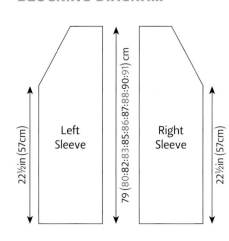

Left Sleeve

Right Sleeve

22½in (57cm)

22½in (57cm)

79 (80:82:83:85:86:87:88:90:91) cm

SIZE

	8	10	12	14	16	18	20	22	24	26	
TO FIT BUST	81	86	92	97	102	107	112	117	122	127	cm
	32	34	36	38	40	42	44	46	48	50	in
LENGTH TO CENTER BACK	19	19	20	20	21	21	22	22	24	24	cm
	7½	7½	8	8	8¼	8¼	8¾	8¾	9½	9½	in
SLEEVE LENGTH (CUFF TURNED BACK)	48	48	48	48	48	48	48	48	48	48	cm
	19	19	19	19	19	19	19	19	19	19	in

YARN

Debbie Bliss Party Angel (Lace weight; 72% superkid mohair, 24% silk, 4% metalized polyester; 219yds/200m, 7/8oz/25g balls)

SHADE 10	3	3	4	4	5	5	5	5	5	5	x25g BALLS

Advent calendar

designed by Belinda Boaden

Start the countdown to a very crafty Christmas in style with our oh-so-cute knitted advent calendar!

This fun advent calendar is designed to use up leftovers of yarn, making it super thrifty. And that gives you the perfect excuse to ask Santa for some lovely new woolly treats this Christmas!

Knit the mini socks plain or striped as you wish, then cross stitch the date onto them in a contrasting color. Charts are given which can be used for cross stitch or Fair Isle embellishment if you wish, so that once the day has been 'opened' the sock can be turned around to show the pattern. The socks use two different heels and two different toes so you can practice your techniques as well as use up bits of yarn. The Fingering and sport weight socks are ideal for stuffing with small items, while the heavy worsted weight sock will hold larger bars of chocolate or gifts. We've even designed a bag to store your socks in, ready for next year!

Great for intermediate knitters

As long as you knit 24 socks it really doesn't matter what weights they all are

The calendar uses up leftovers of yarn, making it super thrifty, and the more yarn colors used, the merrier

The sport weight and fingering weight socks are strong enough for small sweets and tiny gifts

» BASIC HEAVY WORSTED SOCKS

NEEDLES
☐ 4.5mm (UK 7/ US 7) double pointed or circular knitting needles for your preferred method of working in the round

YARN
☐ Each sock uses approx 30yds (27m) of yarn

GAUGE
☐ 18 sts x 24 rounds to 4in (10cm) over st st worked in the round

DRAWSTRING BAG

NEEDLES
☐ 4mm (UK 8/ US 6) double pointed or circular knitting needles for your preferred method of working in the round
☐ Darning needle for embroidery

YARN
☐ Knitted in sport weight or heavy worsted weight yarn. Bag uses approx 120yds (110m) of yarn.

GAUGE
☐ 23 sts x 30 rows to 4in (10cm) over st st worked in the round
☐ 23 sts x 28 rows to 4in (10cm) over Fair Isle patt worked in the round

4-PLY SOCK

Cast on 42 sts. Immediately cast off the first 10 sts to leave a 'string' which will become the loop to hang your sock up in. Arrange the rem 32 sts over your needles and join to work in the round, being careful not to twist and place marker.

Ribbed cuff
* (K2, P2); rep from * to end. Work this round 4 times more. Work now in st st (knitting every round) until sock measures 4cm, ending last round 8 sts before the string/ marker.

Short row heel
Row 1: k15, w&t.
Row 2: p14, w&t.
Row 3: k13, w&t.
Row 4: p12, w&t.
Row 5: k11, w&t.
Row 6: p10, w&t.
Row 7: k9, w&t.
Row 8: p8, w&t.
Row 9: k7, w&t.
Row 10: p6, w&t.
Row 11: k6, k next st with wrap tbl, wrap the next st, turn.
Row 12: p7, p next st with wrap tbl, wrap the next st, turn.

Continue working one more st each row, as per rows 12 and 13, until you are back at 32 working sts **.
Continue in st st on all 32 sts from now on until foot measures 3cm.

Toe
*** **Round 1:** *k6, k2tog; rep from * to end. 28 sts
Round 2: *k5, k2tog; rep from * to end. 24 sts
Round 3: *k4, k2tog; rep from * to end. 20 sts
Work 3 rounds plain.
Round 7: *k3, k2tog; rep from * to end. 16 sts
Round 8: *k2, k2tog; rep from * to end. 12 sts
Round 9: *k1, k2tog; rep from * to end. 8 sts
Work 1 round plain.
Rounds 10 and 11: *k2tog; rep from * to end. 2 sts.

Break yarn, thread through rem sts twice and draw up ***.
Darn in ends, sewing the 10 cast-on-cast-off sts from the very beginning to the base of itself to form the loop that you'll hang the socks up with.

SPORT WEIGHT SOCK

Using 4mm needles, cast on 34 stitches. Cast off the first 10 stitches to leave a 'string' to hang the sock up with. Arrange the rem 24 sts over your needles and join to work in the round, being careful not to twist and place marker.

Ribbed cuff

* (K1, P1); rep from * to end. Work this round twice more. Work now in st st. knitting every round until sock measures 2in (5cm), ending last round 6 sts before the string/ marker.

Short row heel

**Row 1: k11, w&t.
Row 2: p10, w&t.
Row 3: k9, w&t.
Row 4: p8, w&t.
Row 5: k7, w&t.
Row 6: p6, w&t.
Row 8: k5, w&t.
Row 9: p4, w&t.
Row 10: k4, knit the next st with its wrap tbl, wrap the next st, turn.
Row 11: p5, purl the next st with its wrap tbl, wrap the next st, turn.

Continue working one more st each row, as per rows 10 and 11, until you are back at 24 working sts **.
Continue in st st on all 24 sts from now on until foot measures 1⅛in (3cm), again finishing the last round 6 sts before the string/ marker.

Toe

*** Round 1: *k1, ssk, k6, k2tog, k1; rep from * once more. 20 sts
Round 2: Knit.
Round 3: *k1, ssk, k4, k2tog, k1; rep from * once more. 16 sts
Round 4: Knit.
Round 5: *k1, ssk, k2, k2tog, k1; rep from * once more. 12 sts
Round 6: Knit.

Graft remaining toe sts together ***. Darn in ends, sewing the 10 cast-on-cast-off sts from the very beginning to the base of itself to form the loop that you'll hang the socks up with. »

> **TIP**
> If you are using double pointed needles, it can be easier to cast onto a straight needle of the same size. Then divide among the DPNs.

It's up to you how you display your advent socks – use an old branch of wood as we have done – or why not hang them on a mini Christmas tree?

You can knit motifs into the bag using stranded colorwork, or stitch them on later

BASIC HEAVY WORSTED SOCK

Using 4.5mm dpns, cast on 44 stitches. Cast off the first 16 stitches to leave a 'string', which will become the loop to hang the sock up with.
Arrange the rem 28 sts over your needles and join to work in the round, being careful not to twist and place marker.

Ribbed cuff

*(K2, P2); rep from * to end. Work this round 3 times more *. Work now in st st (so knit every round) until sock measures 8cm, ending last round 7 sts before string/ marker.

Heel flap

** **Next row (RS):** k14, turn. Work on these 14 sts only for the heel.
Next row: sl1 p-wise, p13, turn.

Row 1: sl1 p-wise with yarn in back, k13.
Row 2: sl1 p-wise with yarn forward, p13.
Repeat these 2 rows 3 times more.

Turn heel

Row 1 (RS): k7, ssk, k1, turn.
Row 2 (WS): sl1 p-wise, p1, p2tog, turn.
Row 3: sl 1 p-wise, k2, ssk, k1, turn.
Row 4: sl 1 p-wise, p3, p2tog, p1, turn.
Row 5: sl 1 p-wise, k4, ssk, k1, turn.
Row 6: sl 1 p-wise, p5, p2tog, p1.
8 sts now on ndl and all sts worked.

Gusset

Knit across 8 heel sts, and pick up and knit 5 sts along edge of heel, work across 14 instep sts, pick up and knit 5 sts along rem side of heel flap, k first 4 sts of heel again. 32 sts (18 heel sts, 14 instep sts). Each round now beings at the center of the heel.

Round 2: Knit 6, k2tog, k1, knit 14, k1, ssk, knit to end, 30 sts.
Round 3: Knit all sts.
Rep rounds 2 and 3 once more, 28 sts rem. Work in rounds of st st now on these 28 sts until foot portion (from end of heel) measures approx. 2in (5cm).

Toe

***Work 1 further round in st st, ending 7 sts before end of round.
Round 1: *k1, ssk, k8, k2tog, k1; rep from * once more. 24 sts
Round 2: Knit.
Round 3: *k1, ssk, k6, k2tog, k1; rep from * once more. 20 sts
Round 4: Knit.
Round 5: *k1, ssk, k4, k2tog, k1; rep from * once more. 16 sts
Round 6: Knit.
Round 7: *k1, ssk, k2, k2tog, k1, rep from * once. 12 sts
Round 8: Knit.

Graft remaining toe sts together ***.
Darn in ends, sewing the 16 cast-on-cast-off sts from the very beginning to the base of itself to form the loop that you'll hang the socks up with.

DRAWSTRING BAG

Note: Because the bag is worked from the bottom up in the round if you wish to add motifs in stranded colorwork, (Fair Isle technique) you can work from the bottom of the chart upwards as normal, reading all chart rounds from right to left.

Using 4.5mm nds and sport weight yarn, cast on 90 sts using the Turkish Cast on or Judy's Magic cast on.
Place marker for start of round and work in rounds of st st for approx 7 ⅞in (20cm).

Eyelet round: * k6 yo, k2tog, rep from * to last 6 sts, k6. Work a further 2 rounds st st.
Next round: *(k1, p1); rep from * to end. Work in rib as set for ¾in (2 cm), cast off loosely and evenly in rib.

Cast on 3 sts on a dpn.
Using a second dpn, knit 3 sts, place 2nd dpn in left hand and take yarn from end of sts to the start and knit again without turning.
Cast off after 19½in (50cm). Thread through eyelet holes.

NOTES

If you wish to knit the patterns, or the numbers into the sock rather than duplicate stitching or cross stitching them on later remember you will need to work from the top of the chart downwards rather than the bottom of the chart upwards as would be usual. Numbers will have to be worked upside down and right to left - in other words if you were knitting '24' in you would need to begin with the upside down '4' and then move onto the upside down '2'. Adding them afterwards means it's easier to work them both in different colors if you wish.

For Contrast Heel / Toe sock, work sections between ** to ** and *** to *** in your chosen contrast color.

For Striped sock, work as for Contrast Heel / Toe sock but after you have knitted the ribbed cuff work in stripes of 3 rounds each, beginning and ending with a contrasting color from the ribbing, work the heel (** to **) in the same solid color as the ribbed cuff, work foot again in stripes of 3 rounds beginning with the same color as you worked the heel in and work toe section (*** to ***) in the same color as heel / ribbed cuff.

SPECIAL ABBREVIATIONS

w&t: wrap and turn. Bring yarn fwd under needle, sl 1 st (purlwise) off the left hand needle, yarn back, return slipped st to left needle, turn work, work row as instructed. When the wrapped st is eventually worked knit/purl the wrap with the st together.

CHARTS

Numbers

Zig zag

Snowflake

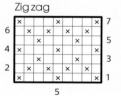

Xmas tree

THE KNITTER
This project was originally featured in *The Knitter*.

KEY

| ☒ | Yarn A |
| ☐ | Yarn B |

Santa hat

designed by Kirstie McLeod

The loopy cuff and pom-pom on Kirstie's hat is so much fun and the sequins add festive sparkle – they're in the yarn, saving you lots of sewing. The loopy stitch is easy – give it a try!

CUFF

Cast on 20 sts using 5mm needles and yarn A.

Row 1 (WS) Knit.

Row 2 (RS) K1, * K1 - (keeping the st on the left-hand needle, bring yarn to the front, wrap yarn round left thumb to form a loop, take the yarn back, knit the st on the left-hand needle again, yo right-hand needle and then pass the 2 sts back over the yo), K1; rep from * to last st, K1.

Row 3 (WS) Knit.

Row 4 (RS) K1, *K1, K1 - (keeping the st on the left hand needle, bring yarn to the front, wrap yarn round left thumb to form a loop, take the yarn back, knit the st on the left-hand needle again, yo right-hand needle and then pass the 2 sts back over the yo); rep from * to last st, K1.

Rep these 4 rows until knitting meas 21½in (55cm) ending with a row 1 or 3. **Cast off.**

HAT

With the RS of the cuff facing, using 5mm needles and yarn B, pick up and K46 sts evenly along the side edge of the cuff.

Row 1 (WS) Pfb into every st. [92 sts]

Row 2 Knit.

Row 3 Purl.

Cont in st st until 7 rows worked, ending with a P row.

Next row *K21, k2tog; rep from * to end of row. [88 sts]

Starting with a P row, st st 3 rows.

Next row *K20, k2tog; rep from * to end of row. [84 sts]

Starting with a P row, st st 3 rows.

Cont to decrease in this fashion until 56 sts remain.

Next row (WS) Purl

Next row K12, k2tog; rep from * to end of the row.

[52 sts]

Rep these 2 rows until 4 sts rem.

POM-POM

Change to yarn A.

Row 1 (WS) Knit.

Row 2 and every alt row (RS) As row 2 of the cuff.

Row 3 (WS) Kfb into each st. [8 sts]

Row 5 As Row 3. [16 sts]

Row 7 K1, kfb; rep from * to end of row. [24 sts]

Row 9 Knit.

Row 11 K1, k2tog; rep from * to end of row. [16 sts]

Row 13 K2tog, to end of row. [8 sts]

Row 15 As Row 13. [4 sts]

Cast off.

FINISHING

With RS facing and starting at cuff, sew along the seam using a matching thread. When you reach the pom-pom turn the right way out, stuff with a little of the leftover yarn A and sew the seam closed. Fold over the cuff and slip stitch the sides together. Weave in all loose ends.

Berry wreath

designed by Kirstie McLeod

**THIS PROJECT
WAS STITCHED USING**

Wendy, Nina* (19% wool, 72%
acrylic, 9% polyester, 3½oz/100g,
13yds/12m)
2 balls of Green Eyes (3060)
NEEDLES

A pair of 6mm needles
YOU WILL NEED

A 12in (30cm) diameter
polystyrene ring

W e just love this yarn! If you're thinking it looks a bit adventurous for you, fear not – there's a how-to video on YouTube – go to http://bit.ly/sk-100-nina. You'll get a great effect for scarves too!

Note: Nina is constructed in a different way than other yarns. The yarn emerges from a black mesh to form a fringe. The black mesh is used to knit and purl through.

Slip 8 mesh loops onto a 6mm needle.
Row 1 Knit each loop, by knitting through the loop on the needle.
Row 2 Purl each loop, by purling through the loop on the needle.
Repeat these 2 rows until the knitting measures 39in (100cm).
Cast off.

FINISHING
With some sport weight yarn, wrap the the knitting around the polystrene ring and sew in place, fastening off any loose ends.
Attach small Christmas decorations with long pins or by sewing them in place.

The shaggy yarn in shades of green makes fab foliage

Tree hangings

designed by Jane Burns

BAUBLE

THIS PROJECT WAS STITCHED USING
Cygnet, Wool Rich fingering
(75% wool, 25% polyamide,
1¾oz/50g, 224yds/205m)
1 ball of each: Geranium (2185),
Holly (0204), Cream (1992)
NEEDLES
2½mm double-pointed needles
YOU WILL NEED
Toy stuffing, 'Red' ribbon with
white saddle stitching.

Cast on 16 sts using 2½mm DPNs and Geranium yarn, then join into the round taking care not to twist. Work in stocking stitch throughout (all rounds Knit), shaping on the following rounds:

Round 1 *K1, kfb; rep from * to end. [24 sts]

Round 4 *K2, kfb; rep from * to end. [32 sts]

Round 7 *K3, kfb; rep from * to end. [40 sts]

Round 10 *K4, kfb; rep from * to end. [48 sts]

Round 13 *K5, kfb; rep from * to end. [56 sts]

Rounds 14–23 Work rows 1–10 of Chart (below).

Round 24 *K5, k2tog; rep from * to end. [48 sts]

Round 27 *K4, k2tog; rep from * to end of round.

Round 30 *K3, k2tog; rep from * to end of round.

Round 33 *K2, k2tog; rep from * to end of round.

Round 36 *K1, k2tog; rep from * to end of round.

Leave a long tail of yarn, then thread tail through darning needle and through each remaining st. Stuff the bauble then pull tight to close.

Cut a 15cm length of ribbon, fold in half and sew flat at join, sew to top of bauble.

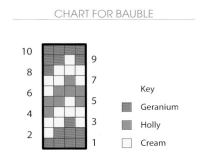

CHART FOR BAUBLE

Key
- Geranium
- Holly
- Cream

MINI JUMPER

THIS PROJECT WAS STITCHED USING
Cygnet, Wool Rich fingering
(75% wool, 25% polyamide,
1¾oz/50g, 224yds/205m)
1 ball of each: Geranium (2185),
Holly (0204),
Cream (1992)
NEEDLES
2½mm needles
YOU WILL NEED
'Red' ribbon with
white saddle stitching.

FRONT

Cast on 18 sts using 2½mm needle and Holly yarn. Use the cable cast-on method.

Row 1 *K1, P1; rep from * to end.

Row 2 *P1, K1; rep from * to end.

Repeat rows 1 and 2 three times in total. Work rows 1–18 from chart (overleaf).

NECK SHAPING IN CREAM

Row 1 K6, cast off next 6 sts, K5 (6 sts rem each side of neck).

Row 2 P6, cast on 6 sts, P6.

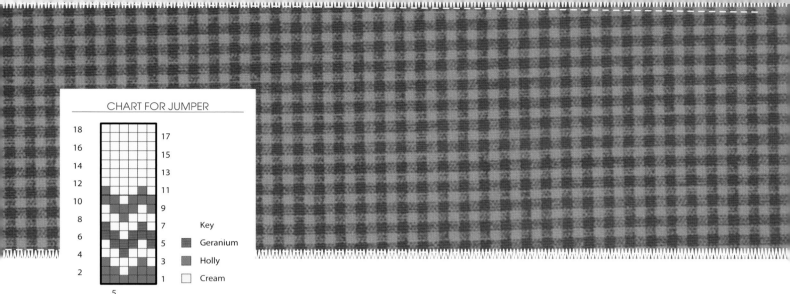

CHART FOR JUMPER

18		17
16		15
14		13
12		11
10		9
8		7
6		5
4		3
2		1
	5	

Key

■ Geranium
▨ Holly
□ Cream

BACK

Work rows 18-1 from Chart (tip: turn the Chart upside down!).
Row 19 *K1, P1; rep from * to end.
Row 20 *P1, K1; rep from * to end.
Repeat rows 19 and 20 three times in total.
Cast off.

SLEEVES (MAKE TWO)

Cast on 14 sts using 2½mm needles and Holly yarn.
Row 1 *K1, P1; rep from * to end.
Row 2 *P1, K1; rep from * to end.
Work rows 1 and 2 once more.
Change to Cream yarn.
Row 5 Knit.
Row 6 Purl.
Row 7 K4, m1, K6, m1, K4. [16 sts]
Row 8 Purl.
Row 9 K4, m1, K8, m1, K4. [18 sts]
Rows 10, 12, 14 and 16 Purl.
Rows 11, 13 and 15 Knit.
Cast off.

With WS facing fold the sleeves in half, then sew underarm seam to form sleeve. With WS facing fold the jumper body in half and sew the ribbing at the sides. Place the sleeves just inside the jumper and sew in place, then sew jumper side seam closed.
Cut a 6in (15cm) length of ribbon, fold in half and sew flat at join, then sew to center back of jumper.

SANTA HAT

THIS PROJECT WAS STITCHED USING
Cygnet, Wool Rich fingering (75% wool, 25% polyamide, 1¾oz/50g, 224yds/205m)
1 ball of each: Geranium (2185), Cream (1992)
NEEDLES
2½mm double-pointed needles
YOU WILL NEED
'Red' ribbon with white saddle stitching.

Cast on 40 sts using 2½mm DPNs and Cream yarn using cable cast on method, then join into the round taking care not to twist sts.
Rounds 1-13 Knit.
Change to Geranium yarn.
Rounds 14-25 Knit.
Round 26 (K8, k2tog) 4 times. [36 sts]
Rounds 27-30 Knit.
Round 31 (K7, k2tog) 4 times. [32 sts]
Rounds 32-33 Knit.
Round 34 (K6, k2tog) 4 times. [28 sts]
Rounds 35-36 Knit.
Round 37 (K5, k2tog) 4 times. [24 sts]
Rounds 38-39 Knit.
Round 40 (K4, k2tog) 4 times. [20 sts]
Round 41 Knit.
Round 42 (K3, k2tog) 4 times. [16 sts]
Round 43 Knit.
Round 44 (K2, k2tog) 4 times. [12 sts]
Round 45 Knit.
Round 46 (K2tog) 6 times. [6 sts]
Round 47 (K2tog) 3 times. [3 sts]

Leave a long tail, then, using a darning needle, thread the tail through the remaining sts on the needle and pull tight to close the top of the hat. Darn in ends and make small pom-pom for the top.

Fold the top of the hat over for the authentic Santa look!
Fold the brim back in half and sew in place, cut a 6in (15cm) length of ribbon, fold in half and sew flat at join, then sew to back of hat.

SANTA BOOTS

THIS PROJECT WAS STITCHED USING
Cygnet, Wool Rich fingering (75% wool, 25% polyamide, 1¾oz/50g, 224yds/205m)
1 ball of each: Cream (1992), Grey Mix (0044)
NEEDLES
2½mm needles
YOU WILL NEED
'Red' ribbon with white saddle stitching.

BOOT (MAKE 2)

Cast on 22 sts using 2½mm needles using Grey mix yarn.
Row 1 Purl.
Row 2 *K1, kfb; rep from * to last 2 sts, (kfb) twice.
Rows 3, 5, 7 and 9 Purl.
Rows 4, 6 and 8 Knit
Row 10 K13, (k2tog) 4 times, K13. [30 sts]
Row 11 Purl.
Row 12 K11, (k2tog) 4 times, K11. [26 sts]
Row 13 Purl
Row 14 K9, (k2tog) 4 times, K9. [24 sts]
Rows 15, 17, 19, 21, 23 and 25 Purl.
Rows 16, 18, 20, 22 and 24 Knit.
Change to Cream yarn.
Row 26 Knit.
Rows 27-38 Knit.
Cast off.

This colorful bauble is knitted in the round.

Finish off this fun Santa hat with a fluffy pom-pom.

This jolly jumper uses clever construction for an easy finish.

Our lollipop looks good enough to eat.

Santa's boots look just the thing to protect him from the cold.

Practise your picot edgings with our cute striped sweet.

HOW TO USE THE CHARTS

Start at the bottom right-hand corner. Read right side rows from right to left and wrong side rows from left to right. A row of squares represents a row of knitting.

With WS facing, fold boot cuff in half and oversew the white boot cuff to inside of the boot, then sew side seam of boot. Cut a 6in (15cm) length of ribbon, fold in half and sew to the inside of each of the boots to hang as a pair from the tree.

STRIPED SWEET

THIS PROJECT WAS STITCHED USING
Cygnet, Wool Rich fingering (75% wool, 25% polyamide, 1¾oz/50g, 224yds/205m) 1 ball of each: Cream (1992), Grey Mix (0044)
NEEDLES
2½mm needles
YOU WILL NEED
'Red' ribbon with white saddle stitching.

Cast on 26 sts using 2½mm needles Geranium yarn and cable cast-on.
Row 1 Knit.
Row 2 Purl.
Repeat rows 1 and 2 once more.

PICOT EDGE
Row 5 *K2tog, yo; rep from * to last 2 sts, K2. [26 sts]
Starting with a purl row, work 9 rows of st st.
Row 11 *K1, k2tog; rep from * to last 2 sts, K2. [18 sts]
Starting with a purl row, work 5 rows in st st.
Continuing in st st, work the following stripe sequence:
*2 rows in Cream
2 rows in Geranium*
Repeat from * to * 4 times.
Work 2 rows in white.

Continue in Geranium to end of piece.
Rows 1-4 St st.
Row 5 *K1, kfb; rep from * to last 2 sts, K2. [26 sts]
Starting with a purl row, work 9 rows in st st.
Row 11 *K2tog, yo; rep from * to last 2 sts, K2. [26 sts]
Rows 12-14 Starting with a purl row st.
Cast off.

Fold at picot rows, with WS facing and sew in place.
Sew side seams together using mattress st, then stuff the 'sweet' section with toy stuffing. Tie the ends of the sweet closed using yarn. Cut a 6in (15cm) length of ribbon, fold in half and sew flat at join, then sew to back of sweet.

THIS PROJECT WAS STITCHED USING
Cygnet, Wool Rich fingering (75% wool, 25% polyamide, 1¾oz/50g, 224yds/205m) 1 ball of each: Geranium (2185), Cream (1992)
NEEDLES
2½mm double pointed needles
YOU WILL NEED
Clear sewing thread, sewing needle, 'Red' ribbon with white saddle stitching.

LOLLIPOP

Cast on 4 sts using 2½mm DPNs and Geranium yarn.
Knit 1 row, slide these 4 sts to other end of needle, do not turn work.
Rep from * to *, pulling yarn tight across the back of i-cord each time you start a new row. Work cord until it measures 7in (18cm) from cast off.
Using Cream yarn work a 7⅞in (20cm) i-cord as above.
Starting with the Cream i-cord curl into a circle and sew in place using a clear thread, then wrap the Geranium cord around this and continue to spiral the two cords, sewing each round in place as you go.
You should end with a tail of Cream yarn approx 1½in (4cm) long. Secure this in place to form a lolly stick.
Cut a 6in (15cm) length of ribbon, fold in half and sew flat at join, then sew slightly to side (at the back) of the lollipop.

Make a whole tree-full of baubles for a fab display.

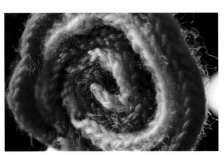

What a clever use of i-cord – simply wrap and stitch.

Cozy cushions

designed by Debora Bradley

YOU WILL NEED

THIS PROJECT WAS STITCHED USING

Yeoman, (bulky weight)
(25% alpaca, 25% wool, 50% acrylic,
14oz/400g, 656yds/600m)
1 cone each of:
Autumn Red (41), Hessian (1)

NEEDLES

A pair of 6½mm knitting needles

YOU WILL NEED

Cushion inners: 14x14in (35x35cm)
for Red cushion, 16x16in (40x40cm)
for Hessian cushion
3 (5) buttons

GAUGE

19 sts and 23 rows to measure
4x4in (10x10cm) over patt using
6½mm needles

ABBREVIATIONS

LN left needle
PB place buttonhole RN
right needle

NOTE: When placing buttonhole, work as folls to make a one-row buttonhole: when you reach where you want the buttonhole to be, bring yarn to front, slip next st purlwise, take yarn to back (this leaves you with a 'bar' of yarn in front of the stitch). Next, *slip 1 st purlwise from LN to RN, and pass the second stitch on the RN over the first st, as you would when casting off.* Repeat from * to * for the required number of stitches – for these cushions cast off two sts in total. Slip the last cast off st from the RN back to the LN as if to knit, and turn the work. Using a cable cast on, cast on one more st than you cast off – 3 sts in this case. Turn work again and slip the first st on the LN on to the RN. Pass the second st on the RN (the extra cast-on st) over the slipped stitch.

Cast on 42 (52) sts using 6½mm needles and Autumn Red 41 (Hessian 1).
Row 1 K2, *P2, K2; rep from * to end of row.
Row 2 P2, *K2, P2; rep from * to end of row.
These two rows form K2, P2 rib pattern. Repeat rows 1 and 2 four more times. [10 rows in total]
Next row Knit.
Next row Purl.
These two rows form stocking stitch. Work in st st until work measures approx 32 or 34in (81 or 87cm) or to fit around your cushion inner (rib to be added will overlap the rib at the start). Work in rib pattern for 4 rows.

SMALLER COVER ONLY

Row 5 (Buttonhole row) K2, P2, K2, P2, PB, P1, K2, P2, K2, P2, PB, P1, K2, P2, K2, P2, PB, P1, K2, P2, K2.

LARGER COVER ONLY

Row 5 (Buttonhole row) K2, P2, K2, P2, PB, P1, K2, P2, PB, P1, K2, P2, PB, P1, K2, P2, PB, P1, K2, P2, K2, P2, K2, PB, P1, K2, P2, K2, P2.

Rows 6-10 Work in the K2, P2 rib pattern.
Cast off in pattern.

Embroider motifs in cross stitch on covers as in photos, following the charts. Place the stitches at the center of chart at the center of cushion cover (measure both ways and mark centre with a pin to start). Each cross stitch covers 1 knitted 'V' stitch across and 2 vertically.

FINISHING

Fold cushion cover so that the two ribbed ends overlap, and move so that the opening is central at the back. Sew up sides using backstitch. Turn the right way out and sew on 3 (5) buttons. Insert inner and button up!

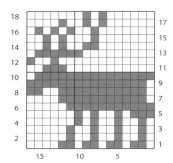

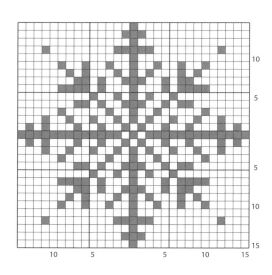

Follow instructions to make this one-row buttonhole.

Make sure you cross all your stitches in the same direction.

This simple reindeer is quick to stitch, but instantly recognizable – everyone loves Rudolph!

HOW TO CROSS STITCH

Each grey block on the chart represents one stitch, and each cross stitch is worked over one knitted stitch across and two up. Secure your yarn at the back, bring the needle up at 1, go down at 2, up at 3, down at 4, then up again in the top left-hand corner of the next 'square' and repeat the process. Alternatively, where you have to work a line of stitches, use half cross stitches from left to right, then double back on yourself. Make sure the top stitches of the crosses all face the same direction.

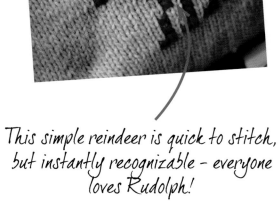